Of the more than 150 cartoonists of the period HST enjoyed most the work of four: Herbert L. Block of the *Washington Post;* Clifford K. Berryman and his son James of the *Washington Star,* and Daniel Fitzpatrick of the *St. Louis Post-Dispatch.* Truman appreciated—and often collected—samples of other artists as well, including Darling, Carey Orr, Silvey Jackson Ray, Cyrus Hungerford, and Frederick Seibel.

The political cartoonist sketches for the general public. Each is subject to personal prejudice and responds to current events rather than analyzing long-range effects. Despite these obstacles the caricaturist keeps the American public informed—and often delightfully so—during Truman's years in public life.

At the end, when Truman was about to return to Independence and to private life, cartoonist Frederick Seibel drew a small and lonely figure walking down the road past the Capitol building captioned: "There goes Harry—he done his damndest."

JAMES N. GIGLIO is professor of history at Southwest Missouri State University, Springfield, a post he has held since 1968.

A native Ohioan, he received his bachelor of arts and master's degrees from Kent State University, and a doctoral degree from Ohio State University, Columbus.

He is a member of the Center for the Study of the Presidency and of the Organization of American Historians.

His present research concerns the Kennedy presidency for the American Presidency Series sponsored by the University of Kansas Press.

Giglio is the author of numerous articles on the American presidents, some of which have appeared in *Presidential Studies Quarterly.*

GREG G. THIELEN is curator of collections at the Springfield Art Museum at Springfield, Missouri. He completed his art studies at Southwest Missouri State University, graduating *cum laude,* and later returned to take a master's degree in social and political history.

Listed in *Who's Who in American Art,* Thielen has authored several museum exhibition catalogues and a variety of articles for art publications such as *The Glaze* and *Art Voices.*

TRUMAN

IN CARTOON AND CARICATURE

IOWA STATE UNIVERSITY PRESS, AMES

TRUMAN

IN CARTOON AND CARICATURE

JAMES N. GIGLIO AND GREG G. THIELEN

© 1984 The Iowa State University Press
All rights reserved

Composed by Typeco, Inc., Des Moines, Iowa 50309
Printed by The Iowa State University Press, Ames, Iowa 50010

First edition, 1984

Library of Congress Cataloging in Publication Data

Giglio, James N., 1939–
  Truman in cartoon and caricature.

  Includes index.
  1. Truman, Harry S., 1884–1972–Cartoons, satire, etc. 2. American
wit and humor, Pictorial. I. Thielen, Greg G., 1940–   II. Title.
E814.G52   1984   973.918′092′4   84–9088
ISBN 0–8138–1806–0

Contents

PREFACE   vi

INTRODUCTION   ix

REPOSITORIES   xiv

APPRENTICESHIP   3

RECONVERSION   14

1948 ELECTION   37

FAIR DEAL   65

COLD WAR   97

PRESIDENT EMERITUS   130

Selected Bibliography   165

THIS BOOK is meant for the general public. We hope that it fulfills an interest in our thirty-third president in the centennial year of his birth. Our intent is for readers to understand more clearly, to laugh a little, to shake their heads occasionally in disbelief, to reminisce a lot, and perhaps sometimes even to "give-em-hell" with HST.

We trust that historians will also find the book useful, for it relies on an unconventional source. The political or editorial cartoon is a democratic art form that reflects the feelings of the community as much as it does the artist and the publication. It furnishes further insights into how society perceives public figures and issues. Hence the political cartoon provides an additional prism through which to view Harry Truman and his presidency. We were particularly impressed with the attention cartoonists gave to matters that historians deem insignificant yet sometimes ignored those things that historians think consequential. We also found that the cartoons portray a multifaceted Truman. They project his courage, tenacity, impulsiveness, frustration, stubbornness, and petulance—above all, his humanity.

If the cartoons fail to depict Truman as the great president that evaluations by historians assume, it is not his or the cartoonists' fault. It is instead due to the nature of the art. Cartoonists respond to immediate events rather than analyze long-range effects. Their audience is the general public, not the scholar. They are subjected to their own prejudices and those of their editors, most of whom were hostile to the Democratic party during Truman's time. Despite these obstacles, the political cartoonists kept the American public informed, sometimes delightfully so, during HST's presidency.

vi

Preface

Nearly all of the 263 cartoons in this book were photographed from original drawings. The originals not only ensured a better photographic image, but they also enabled us to determine the medium the cartoonist used in the drawing. Only when originals of a significant issue or event were unavailable did we resort to clippings from the Truman library or photographic reproductions. These involved no more than twenty-five frames. Almost all of the leading cartoonists are here, along with lesser lights.

We have not intentionally excluded anyone because of ideology. The primary consideration was the availability of the drawing. We also favored Truman's image in the cartoon. In only a few cases did we depart from that consideration. Our other concerns were that the cartoon had something to say about an important issue involving Truman or that it provided an excellent rendering of the president.

The book's format should be self-evident. Each chapter begins with an introductory essay followed by related cartoons and explanatory material. Whenever a cartoon lacked a caption, we created one either by quoting from a written expression in the drawing (designated by quotations) or by extrapolating from the visual message of the cartoon (designated by parentheses).

Many of the cartoons came from the Truman library. We are indebted to the library director and assistant director, Benedict Zobrist and George Curtis, respectively, and to the able and cordial library staff—Dennis Bilger, John Curry, Niel Johnson, Pat Kerr, Erwin Mueller, Elizabeth Safly, and Pauline Testerman. We wish also to thank the State Historical Society of Missouri, the Alderman Library of the University of Virginia, the Cowles Library of Drake University, the Library of Congress, and the University of Iowa Library for use of their drawings. Although it is impossible to mention all of the archivists and librarians who were so courteous and helpful, three names stand out: James Leonardo of the Cowles Library, Gregory Johnson of the Alderman Library, and Robert McCowen of the University of Iowa Library. We wish to thank Art Wood of Rockville, Maryland, for the use of his extensive private collection.

Others also assisted us. Political cartoonists Jon Kennedy (*Arkansas Democrat*), Jim Lange (*The Daily Oklahoman*), and Bob Palmer (*Springfield Leader-Press*) graciously answered our many questions as did Everette Dennis, dean of the University of Oregon School of Journalism. We are also indebted to Dean Dennis and Professor Dominic Capeci, Southwest Missouri State University, for reading portions of the manuscript. Special thanks go to the innumerable political cartoonists and newspapers who generously permitted us to reproduce the drawings, to the Harry S. Truman Library Institute for providing us with a research grant, to Professor Wayne C. Bartee of Southwest Missouri State University for his support, and to Ann Reed who handled much of the permission request work.

Last, but most important, we thank our spouses, Fran and Elaine, who good naturedly tolerated our obsessions with the "cartoon book."

Introduction

ONE SUSPECTS that Harry Truman would have liked this book, for he highly valued the work of political cartoonists. He once wrote that they "express[ed] the opinions of the times better and more succinctly than any of the usual solecisms of columnists and editorial writers." He also believed that cartoonists had a "powerful influence on public opinion." For these reasons he paid attention to their work as he sometimes acknowledged at press conferences.

Moreover, HST appreciated the humor in political cartoons even though it often came at his expense. The humorous exaggerations or distortions, he undoubtedly believed, were part and parcel of the cartoonists' craft. For whatever reason, he accepted it while refusing to tolerate less comical effusions from columnists and editorial writers. Interestingly, Truman's personal correspondence, housed in the Harry S. Truman Library in Independence, Missouri, contains no Truman criticism of editorial cartoonists even though it is replete with HST's damnation of various publishers, columnists, and editors.

HST's correspondence suggests another aspect of his interest in political cartoons. Late in his senatorial career he began to collect cartoons of himself. A few of the leading cartoonists regularly sent him inscribed original drawings, the number of which increased once he became president. Afterward, particularly following the opening of the Truman library in 1957, he often wrote editorial cartoonists, either requesting a recent drawing or ones related to his past. He boasted that he was assembling the largest collection in the country, which later exceeded one thousand originals. His desire for certain cartoons had nothing to do with whether they were flattering. He in fact sometimes surprised cartoonists by asking for cartoons that were personally derogatory. What most of the drawings seemed to have in common is that they represented an unusually good effort or focused on a significant issue.

Of the some 150 editorial cartoonists, HST enjoyed most the work of four cartoonists: Herbert L. Block (*Washington Post*), Clifford K. Berryman and son James (*Washington Star*), and Daniel R. Fitzpatrick (*St. Louis Post-Dispatch*), all Pulitzer Prize winners. By the end of Truman's presidency, Herblock, as he signed his drawings, was the most influential political cartoonist in America. Aside from his favorable view of the Truman administration, he, more than any other political cartoonist, exposed the dangerous Red-baiting of "McCarthyism," a term he himself coined. He also showed his symbol-making ability by devising the tornado-shaped "Mr. Atom Bomb" character frequently appearing in his drawings. A competent draftsman, Herblock was known for his wit and satire. Truman, with typical hyperbole, called him "a great historical artist." "I only wish your drawings could appear in every paper in the country," HST wrote Herblock. Because he cartooned in Washington's only morning newspaper and enjoyed syndication, Herblock received his share of attention.

C. K. Berryman neared the end of his career as HST appeared on the national scene. He was the first cartoonist president of the Gridiron Club, an exclusive Washington press society. Berryman created amazing likenesses. His only concession to caricature was his use of exaggerated head sizes. Like many cartoonists of an earlier day, his drawings were full of detail and labels and were done with pen and ink. Being a Republican, as most cartoonists were, he could be faultfinding about Roosevelt and Truman. There was scarcely a critic more genteel, however; rarely did a Berryman "sting."

Similar in drawing style and political viewpoint, Jim Berryman had become a political cartoonist for the *Star* in 1935 after finishing a drawing for his stroke-afflicted father. He was a better draftsman than C. K., with a more sophisticated use of spatial perspective. Yet his incisiveness remained remarkably subdued. His cartoons of HST, although often critical, were totally without malice. Like his father, who retired in 1949, he sent many humorously inscribed originals to the president. As did other cartoonists, both Berrymans exhibited a sincere fondness for HST that seemed not to have affected their work.

Dan Fitzpatrick, who cartooned Truman before he became a national figure, continued to draw him until Fitzpatrick's retirement in 1957. Ultraliberal on social issues and fiercely opposed to all forms of totalitarianism, Fitzpatrick was sympathetic to Truman's presidency. He relied on the generous use of grease crayon to get his message across. His cartoons could be dark, brooding, powerful statements, particularly during the war years. Known for his splendid symbolism, he often made his points so vividly that captions were not required.

Besides the aforementioned four, other political cartoonists made an impact during the Truman period. Many of them had cartooned for decades prior to the Truman presidency. Included in this category were Jay N. "Ding" Darling (*Des Moines Register*), Carey Orr (*Chicago Tribune*), Silvey Jackson Ray (*Kansas City Star*), Cyrus Hungerford (*Pittsburgh Post-Gazette*), and Frederick Seibel (*Richmond Times Dispatch*), all reared in the nineteenth century. By far the best known, the Pulitzer Prize winning Ding was nationally syndicated up to his retirement in 1949. For years a strong admirer of fellow Iowan Herbert Hoover, he opposed Truman's Fair Deal and internationalist foreign policy. He focused much of his criticism on what he and many other cartoonists considered "excessive" federal spending. Darling's originals were extremely large, complex, and occasionally cluttered. He relied on visual humor and labels as many of the old school did, and he drew with brush and ink, creating a penlike effect after his drawings were reduced for publication. Above all, his excellent caricatures of HST exhibited a light touch that enabled him to make a point without rancor.

Carey Orr, another Pulitzer Prize recipient, also embraced the conservative tradition. Unlike his *Tribune* predecessor, the famed John McCutcheon who dared to disagree with publisher Robert McCormick, Orr followed the *Tribune's* editorial leads that viewed the New Deal-Fair Deal as threats to freedom. Orr was as adamant about the Democratic party's interventionist foreign policy. Conversely, he viewed Wisconsin Senator Joseph McCarthy's anti-Communist shenanigans as public service. If he and his *Tribune* associate, Joseph Parrish, ever composed a pro-Truman cartoon, it is yet to be uncovered. Moreover, they sometimes accentuated their biases by portraying Truman as a diminutive wimp. In style, Orr and Parrish relied primarily on a realistic approach rather than on caricature. Both depended on exaggerated action and humor. They were probably alone in having their cartoons, often in color, displayed on the newspaper's front page.

Although his readership was less extensive, S. J. Ray, of the anti-Truman *Kansas City Star*, deserves recognition for his earlier award-winning work. Ray's realistic pen and ink style resembled that of the *Chicago Tribune* cartoonists, even though his drawings contained more open or negative space and less animation. Too, Ray portrayed Truman and his policies more favorably.

Two other seasoned veterans prevailed as Truman assumed the presidency. In Cy Hungerford's half-century of cartooning, his broad, "easy" style and genial approach remained virtually unchanged. Without the malice of Orr and Parrish, he exaggerated the smallness of HST's physique as he did all politicians whom he enjoyed reducing to size. He seemed equally critical of both Republicans and Democrats. In more than forty years of cartooning, Seibel achieved national prominence for his artistry. His work was characterized by the use of a mascot — a bespectacled little crow bearing a resemblance to its author. Seibel seemed to take no consistent stance on Truman's policies.

Among younger established cartoonists, four others stood out: Bruce Russell (*Los Angeles Herald*), Vaughn Shoemaker (*Chicago Daily News*), Daniel Dowling (*New York Herald-Tribune*), and Gibson Crockett (*Washington Star*), all born in the early twentieth century. Russell and Shoemaker drew similarly. Their caricatures could be exceedingly comical, but they could also adopt a realistic style. In his portrayals of Truman, the Pulitzer Prize winning Russell conformed more to the latter approach. "Shoes" Shoemaker, meanwhile, became a syndicated cartoonist for the *New York Herald-Tribune* in 1951. He is noted for his frequent use of such cartoon techniques as beads of sweat, motion lines, and stars of pain. Dowling, the first president of the Association of American Editorial Cartoonists, patterned his style after "Ding" Darling. His cartoons were full of humorous exaggerations. Dowling's caricatures of HST were particularly amusing. Finally, Gib Crockett, in the tradition of the Berrymans, drew in the portraiture school of cartooning and adopted an independent-leaning Republican posture. His drawings bore a remarkable resemblance to those of Jim Berryman.

Late in HST's career, several young cartoonists also came of age, but their opportunities to draw Truman were limited since he no longer held public office. Born in the 1920s and 1930s, they included William (Bill) Mauldin (*Chicago Sun-Times*), Paul Conrad (*Los Angeles Times*), James Ivey (*Orlando Sentinel-Star*), and William Sanders (*Kansas City Star*). As a group more incisive and liberal in posture, they sought to promote social change. Undoubtedly, the advocacy of Herblock had an impact on some of them. Mauldin, a twenty-three-year-old Pulitzer Prize winning cartoonist while serving in the U.S. Army in 1945, was a classic example of the new school. He frequently promoted civil rights issues during the 1950s and 1960s. These same cartoonists excelled as humorists and relied less on labels and captions. Moreover, they also leaned more to caricature, a prevailing trend since the 1960s.

But did political cartoons in fact have a "powerful influence on public opinion," as HST contended? Was there in Truman's time an equivalent to Thomas Nast, the 1870s cartoonist for *Harper's Weekly,* whose scorching drawings of William Marcy Tweed caused that notorious New York City boss to remark: "Stop them damn pictures"? The only one who came close was Herblock who supposedly caused the Red-baiting Richard Nixon in 1960 to comment: "I have to erase the Herblock image." Other leading Truman era cartoonists, many ending lengthy careers, reverted to more placid cartoon work. They became news illustrators rather than interpreters or molders. Others like Darling or Orr did little more than reflect the conservative viewpoints of their newspapers and their region. Only after Truman's presidency did the powerful work of Mauldin evolve. By the 1970s, the influential efforts of Patrick Oliphant (*Denver Post*), David Levine (*New York Review of Books*), and others followed.

This is not to say that political cartooning lacked quality during the Truman era, a time best understood as transitional. An inordinant number of excellent cartoonists retired in this period to be followed by those who made their mark afterward. Their work speaks for itself.

Repositories

ALUV	Alderman Library, University of Virginia, Charlottesville.
AWC	James Arthur Wood, Jr., Collection, Rockville, Maryland.
CLDU	Cowles Library, Drake University, Des Moines, Iowa.
HSTL	Harry S. Truman Library and Museum, Independence, Missouri.
JFKL	John F. Kennedy Library, Columbia Point, Boston, Massachusetts.
LC	Library of Congress, Washington, D.C.
SHSM	State Historical Society of Missouri, Columbia.
UIL	University Libraries, University of Iowa, Iowa City.

TRUMAN

IN CARTOON AND CARICATURE

1

APPRENTICESHIP

HARRY S. TRUMAN'S background seems as uneventful as that of most American presidents. He was born in a small frame house on May 8, 1884, in the western Missouri village of Lamar. A decade previously, Herbert Clark Hoover had emerged from similar modest circumstances in West Branch, Iowa. Harry's parents, John Anderson and Martha Ellen, produced two other children, Vivian and Mary Jane. Although family relationships were warm, life was often a struggle for the Trumans. They moved frequently in those early years as John sought economic betterment. After several years of farming, the family in 1890 settled in Independence, Missouri, about twelve miles east of Kansas City.

In Independence Harry benefited from the educational opportunities a community that size provided. There, in a Presbyterian Sunday school class, he met the "most beautiful girl" he had ever seen. The shy seven-year-old only occasionally talked to Bess Wallace, later carrying schoolbooks home for her. Twenty-eight years after that first meeting, they were married. Their engagement survived years of economic and physical uncertainty, including his participation in World War I.

Truman's military service had a profound effect on him. A studious child whose poor eyesight kept him from sports and an appointment to West Point, Harry compensated by playing the piano and reading almost every book in the local library. His father's financial reversals later prevented him from attending college. Besides working for the railroad, he clerked in two Kansas City banks until his parents moved to the family farm near Grandview, southwest of Independence. He eventually assumed full responsibility of the operation after his father's death in 1914. By then HST had matured. Hard work had toughened him, and he had become more outgoing after joining the Democratic party, the Masons, and the National Guard.

HST's developing ability to work with people received its greatest challenge during the war. After his artillery regiment arrived in France in 1918, he became commander of Battery D, composed mainly of boisterous Irish and German Catholics from Kansas City. Because of his firm but caring leadership, "Captain Harry" won their friendship for life. Unlike so many other Americans, he returned home stronger for that ordeal. For the remainder of his life, while detesting war, HST nevertheless idealistically believed that military training would benefit all young men as it had him.

Following his return in 1919, the newly married Truman and an army buddy, Eddie Jacobson, started a men's furnishings store in Kansas City. Business flourished until the depression of 1921-1922 forced them out. The conservative fiscal policies of the Harding administration, HST believed, contributed to the store's collapse and in effect strengthened his allegiance to the Democratic party. Refusing to declare bankruptcy, he struggled for almost twenty years to successfully retire his indebtedness.

Immediately prior to the store closing, Jim Pendergast, a World War I comrade and nephew of Boss Tom, induced the personable Truman to run for county judge (in Missouri an administrative office) of eastern Jackson County where HST had many friends. For two years Harry served in that capacity, and in 1926, with Boss Tom Pendergast's support, he was elected presiding judge of Jackson County. For the next eight years Judge Truman helped improve the county road network, construct a stately courthouse in downtown Kansas City, and provide jobs for the needy. He learned to work with organized labor and blacks. While willing to cooperate with the Pendergast organization on patronage matters, he refused to do anything against the public interest. Pendergast grudgingly came to respect Truman's independent ways.

In 1934, after other choices had not materialized, Boss Tom pushed the fifty-year-old Truman into the United States Senate race that he, of course, won. For the first time, he now became the subject of political cartoons outside of Kansas City. And as Missouri's junior senator, he became a loyal New Dealer, supporting FDR's recovery and relief programs. He even defended Roosevelt's attempt to "pack" the Supreme Court. Because of Truman's loyalty, the Roosevelt administration often took him for granted. Many in the Senate respected him less, privately referring to him as the "senator from Pendergast."

Consequently, reelection in 1940 seemed unlikely. By then Tom Pendergast was in federal prison for income tax evasion. In the Senate primary race, the ambitious and popular governor, Lloyd Stark, proprietor of a famous Missouri nursery, challenged Truman with support of the Roosevelt administration. Maurice Milligan, the Kansas City district attorney responsible for Pendergast's conviction, also opposed Truman. HST's friends, who had encouraged Milligan to make the race, hoped that the district attorney would divide the "good government" vote with Stark. Fighting for his political life, HST traversed the state by automobile, strongly defending his record. He managed to win the primary by a scant 8,000 votes. That fall he was reelected. Eight years later he again defied the "experts" in a hard-fought presidential campaign.

HST's second Senate term proved more productive, especially after World War II began. Missourians soon informed him of gross profiteering by contractors engaged in construction projects at Fort Leonard Wood. He visited the location himself where his worst suspicions were confirmed. Barracks, mess halls, and other buildings cost three or four times more than they should have. He found waste everywhere. Suspecting that such improprieties existed in other states, Truman introduced a Senate resolution requesting an investigation.

The Special Committee to Investigate the National Defense Program began its work in early 1941. It was commonly known as the Truman committee in deference to its energetic and judicious chairman. Truman, without disrupting the war effort, vigorously exposed the waste, wrongdoing, and obstruction affecting the nation's defense program. The committee probably saved the country $15 billion. In the process, as political cartoons clearly reveal, HST became a national figure by 1942. The following year he made the cover of *Time*.

In early 1944 the press mentioned HST as a possible vice-presidential candidate. By then Henry Wallace, FDR's idealistic vice-president, had antagonized city bosses, the South, and conservatives. Most importantly, he had little rapport with the Senate whose postwar support the president badly needed. Along with Truman, former Senator Jimmy Byrnes (South Carolina) and Supreme Court Justice William O. Douglas emerged as challengers. Of the three, Truman least wanted the nomination, for he enjoyed being senator. Nonetheless, FDR selected him probably because of his labor backing, his acceptance among both liberal and conservative Democrats, and his growing influence in the Senate. There is no evidence, however, that a weary and sickly Roosevelt thought Truman more presidential. That fall HST campaigned in eighteen states. His greatest impact came in the South where the Democrats won overwhelmingly. Although he had not yet developed a recognizable style, Truman gained valuable experience that would prove useful in 1948.

As vice-president, HST served less than three months. His efforts to improve relations between the Senate and the presidency met with only modest success. He spent the remainder of his time attending to ceremonial responsibilities since FDR was either ailing or away from Washington much of the time. Truman surely must have suspected that the president would not survive his fourth term. Having no desire to be president, he probably put such thoughts aside.

Fig. 1.1. *Fishing Way Out in the Middle.* Silvey Jackson Ray, ink, 1934. *Kansas City Star,* HSTL.

The earliest available Truman cartoon, portraying the candidates in the 1934 Democratic senatorial primary. HST's two opponents are Congressmen J. L. Milligan of Richmond and John C. Cochran of St. Louis.

Fig. 1.2. *"You're going to Grow . . . "* Dale Beronius, ink, 1937. *Kansas City Star,* HSTL.

HST supports FDR's proposal to enlarge the Supreme Court membership (with liberals) in order to uphold the constitutionality of New Deal legislation.

Fig. 1.3. *No Place for a Kiddie Car.* Daniel Fitzpatrick, ink, crayon, and opaque white, 1940. *St. Louis Post-Dispatch,* HSTL.

The kiddie car cartoon was a Truman favorite. He later hung it in the White House oval office corridor. Fitzpatrick gave Truman little chance of winning the 1940 senatorial primary against Stark and Milligan.

Fig. 1.4. *Hot on the Trail.* John Baer, ink, c. 1941. *Labor,* HSTL.

By 1941 Truman was making a name for himself as his committee began its investigations of the defense program. His experience as a Jackson county judge made him particularly qualified to detect chicanery and waste.

NO TELLING WHAT THEY'LL FIND IF THEY KEEP DIGGING.

Fig. 1.5. *No Telling What They'll Find If They Keep Digging.* Clifford Kennedy Berryman, ink (photostatic reproduction), 1941. *Washington Star,* HSTL.

The Truman committee probe of Wolf Creek Ordnance Plant construction revealed all sorts of extravagance. With Senator Truman is Democratic Senator James Mead (New York), a committee member.

Fig. 1.6. *"What's This All About, Senator?"* Clifford Kennedy Berryman, ink (photostatic reproduction), 1941. *Washington Star,* HSTL.

HST's committee also settled labor disputes that jeopardized the defense effort. In the spring of 1941 John L. Lewis called a national coal strike after the mine owners failed to provide an approximate 17 percent wage increase for northern miners and a 25 percent boost for southern miners. A key issue involved wage differentials between the two sections. HST pressured the disputants to accept a settlement. In this cartoon, Lewis grasps War Labor Board members who appear powerless before the union leader.

Fig. 1.7. *"This Fellow's Too Big . . . "* Clifford Kennedy Berryman, ink (photostatic reproduction), c. 1943. *Washington Star,* HSTL.

By 1943 Truman supported the 48-hour week for war-related industries despite labor's opposition. Historians have completely ignored this issue. With Truman are General George Marshall and Senator Harry Byrd (Virginia).

Fig. 1.8. *"The Army's a Piker . . . "* James Berryman, ink, 1944. *Washington Star,* HSTL.

In 1944 the Truman committee continued its investigations and reports.

Fig. 1.9. *It Must Have Been an Embarrassing Position for the Groom.* Silvey Jackson Ray, ink, 1944. *Kansas City Star,* HSTL.

FDR characteristically led other vice-presidential candidates to believe they had his endorsement. Democratic National Chairman Robert Hannegan seems oblivious to Roosevelt's embarrassment.

Fig. 1.10. *The Political Education of a Vice Presidential Candidate.* Jay Norwood (Ding) Darling, ink (photostatic reproduction), 1944. *Des Moines Register,* CLDU.

Political cartoonists since 1934 have linked HST to Boss Tom Pendergast. This 1944 effort came in the midst of the presidential campaign, a few months before Pendergast's death. Risking public criticism, Vice-President Truman flew to Kansas City to attend the funeral. He was never one to turn his back on old friends.

Fig. 1.11. *"If You're Going to Ban Conventions . . . "* James Berryman, ink, 1945. *Washington Star,* HSTL.

HST prepares to assume the vice-presidency as his former opponents, Vice-President Henry Wallace and Jimmy Byrnes, show disappointment.

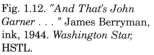

Fig. 1.12. *"And That's John Garner . . . "* James Berryman, ink, 1944. *Washington Star,* HSTL.

Berryman's humor misses the mark, for FDR was serving his final term. Moreover, Truman had no desire to remain vice-president.

Fig. 1.13. *"Everywhere I Go . . . "* Clifford Kennedy Berryman, ink, 1945. *Washington Star,* HSTL.

After Truman replaced Wallace as vice-president, FDR gave Wallace a choice of cabinet seats other than secretary of state. He opted for commerce, a post held by archenemy Jesse Jones. After firing Jones, FDR asked Vice-President Truman to obtain Senate confirmation of the Wallace appointment. HST did so only after much difficulty. In the above cartoon, Senate majority leader Alben Barkley (Kentucky) hands HST the formal request.

Fig. 1.14. *"Better Come Down, Aubrey."* Clifford Kennedy Berryman, ink, 1945. *Washington Star,* HSTL.

HST's efforts to obtain Senate confirmation of Aubrey Williams, a former New Deal administrator, as head of the Rural Electrification Administration failed because of conservative opposition. Truman supposedly advised Williams to give up the losing fight for confirmation.

2

RECONVERSION

ON APRIL 12, 1945, a weary President Roosevelt suddenly succumbed to a cerebral hemorrhage while at Warm Springs, Georgia. While the nation grieved the loss of perhaps its greatest twentieth-century president, a somewhat uncertain Harry Truman took the oath of office. The next day the new president remarked to reporters: "Boys, if you ever pray, pray for me now." The nation was equally uncertain of Truman. After all, next to FDR, the bespectacled, compactly framed, and bow-tied Truman seemed unpresidential. Recognized as a machine politician, he appeared to lack FDR's charisma, vision, knowledge, and independence.

Perhaps because Americans expected so little, Truman initially proved to be a pleasant surprise as president. Immediately after Roosevelt's funeral, he informed Congress that he would pursue his predecessor's policies "to improve the lot of the common people." He responded effectively to war-related problems. He also projected a humble and folksy approach that Americans liked. Consequently, his popularity rating zoomed to 87 percent after one month in the Oval Office.

The honeymoon did not last long. By spring 1946 his popularity had plummeted. A major reason for this was the way he handled reconversion, the process of moving the nation from a wartime to a peacetime society. Not surprisingly, Truman found the war aftermath as difficult as Presidents Lincoln and Harding. His initial problem was with organized labor's insistence on increased wages and fringe benefits following its wartime sacrifices. Management refused union requests, however, causing the auto, steel, and electrical workers to strike. Eventually the railroad and coal miners walked out. The Truman administration succeeded in effecting compromise settlements for most strikes. But when two railroad brotherhoods refused a compromise package and then called a strike, Truman seized the railroads, went on national radio to denounce the labor leaders, and requested Congress to give him authority to draft strikers into the armed forces. Only then did union officials capitulate.

Truman was equally unyielding to John L. Lewis, head of the striking coal miners' union. After Lewis refused several compromises, Truman ordered seizure of the coal mines and secured an injunction against the union. Lewis's violation of the court order cost his union $3,500,000 and him, personally, $10,000 in fines. Thus, despite his generally sympathetic view of organized labor, Truman alienated that element by his recent action. Nevertheless, he argued that he was pursuing national interests. He did not want management passing excessive wage increases on to consumers, thus fueling inflation.

Truman's anti-inflation campaign included extension of wartime price controls into the postwar period, at least until consumer production peaked. The control issue caused the business community and conservatives to turn sharply against Truman. They argued that controls unnecessarily curbed profits and were socialistic. In Congress, Republican Senator Robert Taft (Ohio) led the opposition, forcing Truman to accept price-control compromises that pleased no one, including consumers. Conservatives also attacked Truman for "excessive" federal spending, a popular theme of political cartoonists. Few programs, however, came under as much conservative criticism as price supports for the farmer, a continuation of FDR's agricultural policies.

Truman also incurred the opposition of liberals who resented his not being Roosevelt. Moreover, even though he embraced FDR's New Deal liberalism, he failed to obtain congressional approval of the programs. He also surrounded himself with poker-playing intimates whom pundits labeled the Missouri Gang. As a result, Truman clashed with several Roosevelt appointees, many of whom resigned by 1946. One of the first to depart was Secretary of the Interior Harold Ickes, a crusty old liberal who had once supported Theodore Roosevelt. Ickes resigned after opposing a conservative Truman selection for undersecretary of the navy. Soon afterward, Truman fired Secretary of Commerce Henry Wallace, perhaps the leading liberal visionary, after the latter criticized the increasingly anti-Soviet Truman foreign policy.

Truman again came under fire after purging his home district congressman, Roger C. Slaughter, in the Democratic primaries of 1946. The president felt justified in opposing the reactionary obstructionist who served on the important Congressional Rules Committee. But Truman's dependence on Jim Pendergast to defeat Slaughter soon proved an embarrassment. The Pendergast organization, it was revealed, accomplished the ouster only after engaging in wide-scale voting frauds. That fall the Pendergast candidate lost to a Republican.

It seemed like nothing went right domestically for Truman in 1946. Aside from the aforementioned economic and political difficulties, he was unable to obtain the merger of the three service departments into a single defense department largely because of the opposition of Secretary of the Navy James Forrestal. By autumn newspaper and Republican criticism increased. "To err is Truman" became an often expressed pun. And for the first time in sixteen years, the Republican party gained control of both houses of Congress after a landslide election victory. Many apathetic liberals, blacks, and workers neglected to vote. The lowest point of the early Truman Presidency was reached.

In 1947 the Republican Eightieth Congress seemed to dominate the national government. Truman was forced to adopt a more conciliatory posture as he ended wage and price controls. He also announced that the budget for the next fiscal year would show a slight surplus. But as the year advanced, Truman increasingly exercised his veto power against Republican legislation. The most famous of those actions came against the Taft-Hartley Act, an antilabor bill that outlawed the closed shop and various "unfair" labor practices. Even though Truman favored some union restrictions, he genuinely felt that this law would weaken the trade union movement. As significantly, he knew that a Democratic resurgence in 1948 depended on the support of labor. Indeed, Truman's strong veto message enabled him to regain labor's confidence even though Congress easily secured the necessary two-thirds vote to override the veto. Truman was more successful in vetoing the Republican Eightieth Congress's two tax-cut bills, which he thought inflationary.

By early 1948 Truman embarked upon a positive course as he decided to seek reelection. His liberal advisers had already informed him that he needed to reestablish his liberal credentials to win over the coalition of labor, farmer, black, and Jewish voters that FDR had put together. This backing would be more difficult to secure because Henry Wallace, a prospective third-party candidate, sought the same support.

In January Truman laid the foundation for the fall campaign in his State of the Union address that represented a reaffirmation of his liberal commitments to housing legislation, increased social security and unemployment benefits, and civil rights. Truman had always promoted political and economic equality for blacks. In December 1946 he appointed a President's Commission on Civil Rights. The commission recommended an antilynching law, abolition of the poll tax, desegregation of the armed forces, and several other proposals. By early 1948 Truman had embraced most of the commission report.

Much to the consternation of conservatives, Truman advocated the limited reinstitution of rationing and price controls as anti-inflationary devices. His $39.7 billion budget request for 1948 also brought conservative rebuke for it represented a $2.2 billion increase over 1947. To the Republican opposition, Truman emerged as the ghost of the New Deal past. To Truman, the Eightieth Congress became the Republican "do-nothing" Congress for having ignored his legislative program.

President Truman faced one other domestic clash in early 1948 that Republicans gleefully exploited. It developed when Truman proposed the construction of a balcony outside his second floor White House study. Dubbed the "Truman balcony," traditionalists and architects, including the Commission of Fine Arts, accused Truman of tampering with the architectural integrity of the White House. Truman's press secretary nonetheless announced that construction would soon begin on the forty-foot eliptical balcony. Truman argued that the structure would permit the removal of the old and unattractive first floor awnings. He also suggested that by design the south portico was intended to have a balcony. Only after its construction did criticism end. By then the attractive addition became the biggest tourist attraction in town. But all of this came after the 1948 election.

Fig. 2.1. *His Fighting Spirit Carries On*. James D. Barstow, ink, and crayon, 1945. *General Electric News*, HSTL.

The larger image of FDR is symbolic; HST felt Roosevelt's strong presence. In his first term, he kept a portrait of FDR in the Oval Office. When making a key decision, he sometimes looked at it, wondering, Would he think this is the right thing?

Fig. 2.2. *The Passengers Are Beginning to Sit Back and Relax*. Jay Norwood (Ding) Darling, ink and opaque white, c. 1945. *Des Moines Register*, HSTL.

One of "Ding" Darling's few favorable cartoons of Truman. Ding's Iowa Republicanism made him a frequent administration critic.

Fig. 2.3. *The Answer Seems to Be No.* Daniel Fitzpatrick, ink, crayon, and opaque white, 1945. *St. Louis Post-Dispatch*, SHSM.

Even though HST's popularity had dropped by December 1945, he still had a 63 percent approval rate in the Gallup poll. By June 1946, however, Truman's popularity had plummeted to 43 percent.

Fig. 2.4. *"It Might Head Out to Sea."* Clifford Kennedy Berryman, ink, 1945. *Washington Evening Star*, HSTL.

The main strike threat in September 1945 came from the United Steel Workers of America and the United Automobile Workers. Both unions were seeking a $2-a-day wage increase. Lewis Schwellenbach was HST's inept Secretary of Labor.

Fig. 2.5. (*Something's Knocking in the Engine.*) Karl Kae Knecht, ink, 1945. *Evansville (Indiana) Courier,* HSTL.

The United Automobile Workers struck in November 1945, impeding Truman's reconversion efforts.

Fig. 2.6. *How to Win Friends and Influence People.* Jay Norwood (Ding) Darling, ink, 1946. *Des Moines Register,* UIL.

After Truman's strong actions against the two railroad brotherhoods, A. F. Whitney, president of the Brotherhood of Railroad Trainmen, vowed to use the entire $47 million in the union's treasury to defeat Truman in 1948. Although the above cartoon bears Ding's signature, his main stand-in, Tom Carlisle, probably drew it. The absence of the "x" after the signature suggests that Ding did not do the work.

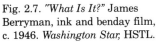

Fig. 2.7. *"What Is It?"* James Berryman, ink and benday film, c. 1946. *Washington Star,* HSTL.

The cartoon fails to impart responsibility for the confused state of price and wage controls by June 1946. Congress had so weakened controls in a one-year extension bill that HST vetoed it, forcing Congress to pass a second bill that contained almost as many loopholes.

Fig. 2.8. *"You've Got 14 Days . . ."* Gib Crockett, ink and benday film, 1946. *Washington Star,* HSTL.

There was a twenty-five day period in July 1946 when no controls existed. Prices jumped tremendously, in some cases doubling, until Congress approved the second bill extending controls.

Fig. 2.9. *Ever Try Walking Down an Ascending Escalator?* Jay Norwood (Ding) Darling, ink, 1947. *Des Moines Register,* UIL.

The cartoonist Darling suggests that HST unrealistically insisted on price reductions despite permitting many other inflationary increases.

Fig. 2.10. *Who Could Have Foretold His Future 25 Years Ago?* Carey Orr, ink and watercolor (clipping from *Chicago Tribune,* copyright © 1947).

The cartoon, in watercolor and prominently displayed on the front page of the *Chicago Tribune,* represented that newspaper's frequent criticism of the president — his administration squandered federal funds.

Fig. 2.11. *The New Deal Chickens Come Home to Roost.* Jay Norwood (Ding) Darling, ink, 1946. *Des Moines Register,* UIL.

Once again a typical reaction to the welfare state. The cartoon ignores Truman's rather tough stand against labor in 1946.

Fig. 2.12. *Within Limits, of Course.* Wills Scott Shadburne, ink, c. 1946. *Springfield (Missouri) Leader and Press,* HSTL.

The cartoon, originating in Truman's home state, views agriculture as immune from criticism during Truman's presidency.

Fig. 2.13. *A Hard Man to Replace.* Jay Norwood (Ding) Darling, ink (photostatic reproduction), c. 1946. *Des Moines Register,* CLDU.

Darling's cartoon is a tribute to the enterprising Ickes but critical of Robert Hannegan, postmaster general and Democratic national chairman, who supposedly thought only of patronage opportunities.

Fig. 2.14. *Trouble among the In-Laws.* Silvey Jackson Ray, ink, 1946. *Kansas City Star,* SHSM.

Although an idealist and utopian, Wallace never courted any radical element in 1946. His basic difference with the president came over foreign policy. He believed that the "get tough with Russia" approach might lead to war. His differences with Secretary of State Jimmy Byrnes on that point caused Truman reluctantly to fire Wallace.

Fig. 2.15. *Another Matter, Mr. President.* Franklin Osborne Alexander, ink and crayon, 1946. *Philadelphia Bulletin,* HSTL.

At the time of Wallace's dismissal, labor strikes were still occurring. Moreover, in the following month (October), John L. Lewis again threatened a coal walkout.

Fig. 2.16. *"Who's Loony Now?"* Clifford Kennedy Berryman, ink, 1946. *Washington Evening Star,* HSTL.

A favorable account of an episode that brought HST nothing but trouble.

Fig. 2.17. *"Anything to Report?"*
James Berryman, ink, 1946.
Washington Star, HSTL.

The major obstacle in a unified
defense system was Secretary of
the Navy James Forrestal who
thought that it would come at
navy's expense. In 1946
Secretary of War Robert P.
Patterson became more
conciliatory to Forrestal, but no
merger agreement materialized.

Fig. 2.18. *"Whew!"* James
Berryman, ink, 1946.
Washington Star, HSTL.

The October 1946 cartoon
catches Truman at one of his
administration's lowest points.
Republican Governor Thomas
Dewey (New York) brought on
the "feud" when he disputed
Republican Senator Robert Taft's
contention that Nazi leaders
failed to receive a fair trial
before the International Military
Tribunal at Nuremburg.

Fig. 2.19. *"Who, Me?"* Clifford Kennedy Berryman, ink, 1946. *Washington Evening Star,* HSTL.

After the devastating election defeat of 1946, Truman had no alternative but to await the convening of the Republican Eightieth Congress.

Fig. 2.20. *Giants and Lilliputians.* Joseph Parrish, ink, 1947. Copyright © *Chicago Tribune,* HSTL.

Another fusillade from one of Truman's greatest nemeses, the *Chicago Tribune.*

Fig. 2.21. *Oh Look What Harry Found in the White House Attic.* Jay Norwood (Ding) Darling, ink (photostatic reproduction), 1947. *Des Moines Register,* CLDU.

Because Truman was initially conciliatory toward the Republican Congress in early 1947, Ding Darling viewed Truman more favorably.

Fig. 2.22. *You Have Our Deepest Sympathy, Son.* M. A. Dunning, ink and opaque white, 1947. *Jacksonville (Florida) Journal,* HSTL.

In the midst of his public tribulations in 1947, Truman's ninety-four-year-old mother, Martha Ellen, died.

Fig. 2.23. *"Let's Put It in a Museum . . . "* Clifford Kennedy Berryman, ink, 1947. *Washington Evening Star,* HSTL.

The actual surplus was $.3 billion from a budget of $38.9 billion. The proud administration official next to HST is Secretary of the Treasury John W. Snyder.

Fig. 2.24. (*President Quixote.*) James Berryman, ink and opaque white, 1947. *Washington Evening Star,* HSTL.

President "Quixote" Truman, as Jim Berryman labels HST, represents a somewhat misleading caricature.

Fig. 2.25. *Easy to See Through Such Magic*. Karl Kae Knecht, ink and crayon, 1947. *Evansville (Indiana) Courier,* HSTL.

As Knecht suggests, Truman's veto was a political necessity for Democratic success in 1948.

Fig. 2.26. *"Did Anybody Get the Number?"* James Berryman, ink, 1947. *Washington Star,* HSTL.

The House vote represented a devastating political defeat for the president. Among the congressmen voting to override the veto was Lyndon Johnson (Texas), while John F. Kennedy (Massachusetts) cast a pro-Truman vote. The Senate voted 68 to 25 against Truman.

Fig. 2.27. *Getting Monotonous.*
Silver Jackson Ray, ink, 1947.
Kansas City Star, SHSM.

Truman's veto against the
Republican tax cut bill in the
summer of 1947 was only one of
his 107 vetoes in that year's two
congressional sessions. In this
period he vetoed more bills than
any president since Grover
Cleveland. In the process,
Truman castigated the
conservative Eightieth Congress
as the worst in history.

Fig. 2.28. *Washington Heat.* Burt
R. Thomas, ink, 1947. *Detroit
News,* HSTL.

Obviously anti-Truman, the
above cartoon compares the
president with V. M. Molotov, the
recalcitrant Soviet Foreign
Minister.

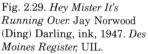

Fig. 2.29. *Hey Mister It's Running Over.* Jay Norwood (Ding) Darling, ink, 1947. *Des Moines Register,* UIL.

Conservatives like Darling believed that HST's opposition to tax relief unnecessarily squeezed the taxpayer. Truman felt that inflation represented a greater threat. In 1948, however, Truman proposed a $40 "cost of living" credit for each taxpayer and dependent.

Fig. 2.30. *All This and Brick Bats Too?* Daniel Fitzpatrick, ink and crayon, 1948. *St. Louis Post-Dispatch,* SHSM.

The above is a sympathetic view of HST's burdens by the liberal *St. Louis Post-Dispatch* cartoonist.

Fig. 2.31. *Bell Ringer.* Herbert Lawrence Block (Herblock), ink and crayon, 1948. Copyright © Washington Post Co., HSTL.

Truman's civil rights message came out one month after his January 1948 State of the Union address. He requested the Congress to legislate his ten-point program on civil rights, which Congress refused to do. Truman was the first twentieth-century president to make such an effort.

Fig. 2.32. *"I Stand Pat!"* Clifford Kennedy Berryman, ink, 1948. *Washington Star,* HSTL.

The implication of the above cartoon is clear. Truman's civil rights commitment could cost him the Democratic South. In early 1948, however, Truman's liberal advisers believed that the South would remain safely Democratic.

Fig. 2.33. *Come Kitty, Nice Kitty.*
Jay Norwood (Ding) Darling,
ink, c. 1948. *Des Moines
Register,* UIL.

When Truman suggested the
selective reinstitution of
rationing in early 1948, Ding
reminded readers of the dangers
of that approach.

Fig. 2.34. *Even Santa Claus
Doesn't Need All That Hair.* Jay
Norwood (Ding) Darling, ink,
1948. *Des Moines Register,* UIL.

The above cartoon proposes that
Truman's 1949 budget needed
considerable Republican
pruning, particularly the
European assistance segment.

Fig. 2.35. *Full House.* Jay Norwood (Ding) Darling, ink, 1948. *Des Moines Register,* UIL.

The proposed 1949 budget ($39.7 billion) once again came under attack, this time for its supposed excesses in welfare allocations. Even though this budget represented a slight increase over the 1948 one, it nonetheless was a far cry from the $67.4 billion proposed budget for 1946.

Fig. 2.36. (*Sidewalk Superintendents.*) Paule Loring, ink and wash, c. 1948. *Evening Bulletin (Providence),* HSTL.

In early 1948 the Eightieth Congress was "bulldozing" Truman's legislative program. The person standing next to HST is J. Howard McGrath, chairman of the Democratic National Committee. The latter would be in charge of the 1948 campaign.

Fig. 2.37. *Just As Good As New.*
Jay Norwood (Ding) Darling,
ink, 1948. Unpublished, UIL.

Truman's populistic railings
against Wall Street and the
special interests invited this
election-year cartoon.

Fig. 2.38. *"Love Me . . . Love My
Balcony!"* Gib Crockett, ink and
crayon, 1948. *Washington Star,*
HSTL.

Whether HST fired the Fine Arts
Commissioners is unrecorded in
the history books. This is just one
example of how editorial
cartoonists sometimes focus on
issues that historians ignore.

3

1948 ELECTION

HARRY TRUMAN'S 1948 election victory was his greatest political triumph. It made him a hero to average Americans as he overcame the prognoses of the leading political analysts and the challenge of the well-financed and meticulously organized Dewey candidacy. Moreover, he had taken his campaign to the people, particularly to laborers, farmers, and those dependent on social security. He traveled over 35,000 miles in a whistle-stop effort that crisscrossed the United States intermittently from June to November. His "give-em-hell-Harry" style became a trademark, almost transforming his political personality and winning him the admiration of future political underdogs who sought to emulate his accomplishment.

The year began with no hint of such success. After Truman's January reaffirmation of Democratic liberalism, rumblings of discontent came from southern leaders who threatened to bolt the Democratic National Convention in July if Truman remained committed to civil rights. Henry Wallace had already declared himself an independent candidate. Calling the Democrats a party of war and depression, Wallace appealed to liberals who wished an alternative to Truman whom they accused of talking like a liberal but acting otherwise. The president could also count on the formidable opposition of the GOP. Dewey, Taft, Governor Earl Warren (California), and former Governor Harold Stassen (Minnesota) loomed as leading contenders. According to a Gallup poll in March, Dewey and Stassen would defeat Truman; Taft would come close.

Truman exhibited his fighting qualities that spring when he brought his program to the people. The pretext of his western tour, which he labeled nonpartisan, was an invitation to deliver the commencement address at the University of California in

June. As the presidential train sped westward, it stopped periodically, enabling the president to speak at prearranged locations. From the train's rear platform, Truman damned the Republican Eightieth Congress's failure to respond to the needs of the people. Observers noted the president had readopted the extemporaneous speaking style that had characterized his senatorial campaigns. As his advisers predicted, he became more effective as he employed colloquialisms and wit to accentuate his points. In the process he lost the monotone and flatness evident in his formal speeches. Thus began the expressive, direct, and brash Truman style. One example of it came at Dodge City where Truman pinpointed the issues: "Are the special privilege boys going to run the country, or are the people going to run it?"

On June 21, three days after Truman's return to Washington, the Republican National Convention convened. Besides adopting a liberal party platform that followed several of Truman's suggested programs, the delegates nominated the moderate Dewey and the liberal Earl Warren as his running mate, both capable administrators of large states. It was a strong ticket and Truman appeared a certain loser.

In order to avert defeat, several Democratic leaders anxiously looked for alternatives to Truman on the eve of the Democratic National Convention. A favorable choice among some liberals and urban bosses was Dwight David Eisenhower. Even though Ike's political views were undetermined, the war leader enjoyed a tremendous popularity. Democratic leaders hoped to exploit that sentiment. Only on the eve of the Democratic National Convention did Eisenhower unequivocally remove himself from the running. Anti-Truman Democrats then feebly attempted a boom for William O. Douglas, the United States Supreme Court Justice.

The Democratic convention assembled in Philadelphia on July 12. Despite an inspirational keynote speech by the old war horse Senator Alben W. Barkley (Kentucky), trouble began the next day over the party platform. Truman's efforts to moderate his civil rights commitments to fit the evasive language of the 1944 plank backfired when northern liberals, led by Hubert Humphrey, Mayor of Minneapolis, fought for a strong civil rights plank. Most of the Alabama and the entire Mississippi delegations walked out. Thus the Dixiecrat party emerged with Governor Strom Thurmond (South Carolina) as its presidential nominee. Soon after, the Progressive party became the vehicle for Wallace's candidacy, further splintering the Democratic party.

The Democrats, meanwhile, unenthusiastically nominated Truman on the first ballot and selected Barkley as his running mate. As the convention ended late that evening, Truman energized the delegates by delivering a spirited address in which he promised: "Senator Barkley and I will win this election and make these Republicans like it — don't you forget that!" Continuing the attack, the president again indicted the Eightieth Congress for ignoring economic controls, aid to education, slum clearance, and other proposals. He enumerated the commitments Republicans had made in their platform to institute housing, social security, and educational assistance legislation. He then announced that he was calling a special session of Congress to enable Republicans to enact their platform. Truman knew only too well that congressional Republicans, representing the party's conservative wing, were unlikely to respond favorably. After their inactivity, he was able to argue that Republicans expediently favored progressive legislation while really opposing it.

Immediately after the convention, Truman finally acted upon an earlier promise by issuing two executive orders: the first sought to end segregation in the armed forces, and the other forbade the civil service from discrimination in governmental hiring. These orders, of course, were in line with the party's liberal civil rights plank. Coming at this time, they underscored Truman's sincerity to the black community.

Truman officially opened his campaign on Labor Day, speaking in Cadillac Square in Detroit. There he chastised the Eightieth Congress for passing the Taft-Hartley Act. If Republican "gluttons of privilege" remain in power and elect a Republican president, he warned, "labor can expect to be hit by a series of body blows — and if you stay at home as you did in 1946, and keep these reactionaries in power, you deserve every blow you get." Dewey, he suggested, represented one of those "with a calculating machine where the heart ought to be."

Truman received a tremendous reception in Detroit. In the weeks ahead he embarked on two major transcontinental trips along with several lesser tours. An estimated six million people heard his more than 350 speeches, many of them delivered from the rear platform of the "Truman Special." In a typical stop he first delivered a rousing attack against the Republican leadership. Then he smilingly introduced Mrs. Truman, whom he called the Boss, and daughter Margaret who bossed the Boss. Finally, the president leaned over the railing to shake hands and exchange pleasantries. While the local band played in the background, the train slowly moved out of the station.

At Dexter, Iowa, clearly GOP country, Truman scored heavily against the Republican opposition. He revealed that the Eightieth Congress had refused to appropriate funds for federal storage bins to hold grain surpluses. With a bumper harvest likely, Midwest farmers feared lower farm prices. Truman's point was clear: The Wall-Street-dominated Republican leadership cared little for farmers or working-class Americans. Truman continued this theme elsewhere, arguing that if Republicans were victorious a depression was likely — a frightening prospect for those who remembered the 1930s. He linked his opponent philosophically with the Republican congressional leadership despite Dewey's advocacy of housing, social security, and other progressive programs.

Dewey, for the most part, ignored Truman's hard-hitting and often misleading barbs. Well ahead in the polls, Dewey assumed the tactics of a prospective winner, one who would avoid controversy and guttersniping. Instead, he adopted a high-minded presidential approach that sought national unity for his expected administration.

Like the press and political analysts, the Dewey headquarters failed to detect the inroads HST made in the campaign's last weeks as audiences and enthusiasm grew at each Truman stop. Instead, the October *Newsweek* magazine poll of fifty leading political writers became the major news as *all* fifty predicted a Dewey victory. Closer to the election, a Gallup poll also projected a Dewey win.

As political cartoonists emphasized, Truman's astonishing victory was in part a tribute to his fighting, unflinching spirit. Throughout those grueling sixteen-hour-day whistle-stops, he had shown himself a scrapper despite the low polls, insufficient campaign funds, and myriad other obstacles. In explaining his victory, the usually unfriendly *New York Sun* editorialized the day after the election: "You just have to take off your hat to a beaten man who refuses to stay licked! . . . Mr. Truman won because this is still a land which loves a scrapper."

Truman also won because his advisers had outlined a sound strategy that enabled him to take advantage of his party's strengths. His recommitment to Democratic liberalism and civil rights won him the labor and black vote. Wallace's inept efforts made it easier. A liberal posture also explains Truman's key inroads in the Midwest where he unexpectedly won Illinois and Iowa. Too, the Dixiecrat strength in the South failed to materialize partly due to the Democrats' southern strategy. There the president, far from talking about civil rights, emphasized the economic gains that the South secured since FDR. As a result, Thurmond won only four southern states. Finally, Truman's strong anti-Soviet foreign policy increased his public support particularly after he responded to the Soviet blockade of Berlin with an airlift.

Moreover, Truman benefited from the fact that most voters were registered Democrats, as was the case since 1932. Many of them entertained thoughts of crossing over, only to change their minds by election day. Others failed to vote, contributing to the low voter turnout in 1948. Nevertheless, the Truman victory once again buoyed Democratic spirits. Much was expected for 1949.

Fig. 3.1. *Political State of the Union.* Silvey Jackson Ray, ink, 1948. *Kansas City Star,* SHSM.

Ray's New Year's Day cartoon anticipates Truman's liberal State of the Union address.

Fig. 3.2. *Direct Appeal.* Leonard D. Warren, ink, crayon, and opaque white, 1948. *Cincinnati Enquirer,* HSTL.

Warren's January drawing portrays a major Truman concern — the November election. In early 1948 the American voter seemed skeptical of Truman.

Fig. 3.3. (*I'm Mild About Harry.*) Karl Kae Knecht, ink and crayon, 1948. *Evansville (Indiana) Courier,* HSTL.

Truman's civil rights message invited this frequent response.

Fig. 3.4. *"I'm Going to Bolt!"* Clifford Kennedy Berryman, ink, 1948. *Washington Evening Star,* HSTL.

In February Berryman did not envision the eventual third-party move.

Fig. 3.5. (*On Top of Everything Else.*) Wills Scott Shadburne, ink, 1948. *Springfield (Missouri) Leader and Press,* HSTL.

The threatened bolt indeed concerned Truman. It caused him to moderate his civil rights program by convention time.

Fig. 3.6. *Overdoing the Razzle-dazzle.* James Berryman, ink, 1947. *Washington Evening Star,* HSTL.

All four potential GOP "ball carriers" concealed their numbers. Of the four HST believed Taft the most formidable.

Fig. 3.7. *All the Doctors Are on Another Case Right Now.* Jay Norwood (Ding) Darling, ink, 1948. *Des Moines Register,* UIL.

As Ding suggests, election politics permeated the national scene in 1948.

Fig. 3.8. *Game to Go on a Campaign Tour?* Daniel Fitzpatrick, ink, crayon, and collage, 1948. *St. Louis Post-Dispatch,* SHSM.

By April Truman decided on a "nonpolitical" western trip in the tradition of many of his twentieth-century predecessors including Presidents Taft and Harding.

Fig. 3.9. *Westward Ho!* Daniel Fitzpatrick, ink and crayon, 1948. *St. Louis Post-Dispatch,* SHSM.

This cartoon is a wonderful example of Fitzpatrick's symbolism. Beginning the western tour on June 4, Truman sought to overcome the political darkness.

Fig. 3.10. *The President Goes into Training* . . . Gib Crockett, ink and benday film, 1948. *Washington Star;* HSTL.

In the spring, Truman's staff suggested a change in speaking style. Charles Ross was HST's press secretary, Clark Clifford was a key senior staff adviser, and Harry Vaughan was a military aide and long-time friend.

Fig. 3.11. *Counting His Chickens.* Jay Norwood (Ding) Darling, ink, 1948. *Des Moines Register;* UIL.

This Ding effort in June is a classic example of "counting the chickens before they are hatched!"

Fig. 3.12. *David and Goliath.*
Jay Norwood (Ding) Darling,
ink, 1948. *Des Moines Register,*
UIL.

Even though the press and
pollsters viewed Truman as an
underdog in the summer of
1948, the Republican Ding
depicts Dewey as David and the
Democratic federal bureaucracy
as Goliath.

Fig. 3.13. *The Ambulance Crew
Will Now Take Over.* Jay
Norwood (Ding) Darling, ink,
1948. *Des Moines Register,* UIL.

The Democratic party's prospects
indeed appeared bleak
immediately after the Republican
National Convention.

Fig. 3.14. *It'll Take More Than a Couple of Juveniles to Break It Up.* Silvey Jackson Ray, ink, 1948. *Kansas City Star,* SHSM.

Leon Henderson and Elliott Roosevelt (FDR's son) represented Democrats who favored a Truman alternative to save the party from a November defeat. For awhile it appeared that HST would face a challenger for the nomination.

Fig. 3.15. *Sorry Harry, It's Everybody for Himself, Now!* Silvey Jackson Ray, ink, 1948. *Kansas City Star,* SHSM.

Another Ray cartoon identifies the Democratic opposition that shunted HST on the eve of the Democratic convention. It included liberals such as Leon Henderson, Senator Claude Pepper (Florida), Jimmy Roosevelt (also FDR's son), urban bosses such as Jacob Arvey (Chicago) and Frank Hague (Jersey City), and much of the southern leadership.

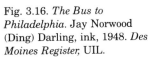

Fig. 3.16. *The Bus to Philadelphia*. Jay Norwood (Ding) Darling, ink, 1948. *Des Moines Register,* UIL.

Possible Democratic alternatives included Eisenhower, William O. Douglas, and Senator Harry Byrd (Virginia). Their cartoon location suggests their order of popularity among Democrats seeking a change. Truman seems not to have noticed.

Fig. 3.17. *The Last Sad Rites*. Jay Norwood (Ding) Darling, ink, 1948. *Des Moines Register,* UIL.

On the eve of the Democratic convention, Ike issued a statement saying that "no matter under what terms, conditions or premises . . . I would refuse to accept" the nomination. In the background of Ding's cartoon, HST, Dewey, Taft, *et al*. appear relieved.

Fig. 3.18. *Light Horse Harry.*
Jesse Taylor Cargill, ink, 1948.
Publisher unknown, HSTL.

Henry Wallace's presidential
candidacy, leading to the
emergence of the Progressive
party in late July, resulted in one
of two Democratic schisms in
1948. Only a small minority of
liberals joined Wallace, however.
Many believed that the Wallace
candidacy would weaken the
Democratic party enough to
ensure Dewey's election.

Fig. 3.19. *He's Over.* Jay
Norwood (Ding) Darling, ink,
1948. *Des Moines Register,* UIL.

Southern opposition to the
Democratic party's liberal civil
rights plank created the other
schism, leading to the States'
Rights Democratic party
(Dixiecrats). If Truman had his
way, the obstacle portrayed in
the above cartoon would not
have been as formidable.

Fig. 3.20. " . . . *They've Already Gone, Howard.*" Clifford Kennedy Berryman, ink, 1948. *Washington Star,* HSTL.

As Berryman suggests, some leading southern Democrats bolted the party. Actually, the number who did was minuscule; southern Democratic leaders were not anxious to lose positions of power. In November the Dixiecrats managed to capture only four states, all in the deep South.

Fig. 3.21. *A Home Run or a Strikeout?* Silvey Jackson Ray, ink, 1948. *Kansas City Star,* SHSM.

HST called the Eightieth Congress into special session on July 26. "Out in Missouri," Truman said, "we call [that day] Turnip Day." In response to the cartoon's caption, one can say that the Turnip session struck out.

Fig. 3.22. *" . . . Let Me at 'Im!"* James Berryman, ink, 1948. *Washington Evening Star,* HSTL.

In July 1948 Truman made the "do-nothing" Eightieth Congress the main issue. He eventually tarred Dewey with the same brush, painting him no differently than Taft and other Republican congressional conservatives.

Fig. 3.23. *"They're Off."* Walt Kelly, ink (photostatic reproduction), 1948. *New York Star,* HSTL.

This is an often reproduced cartoon on the opening of the fall campaign. While Wallace carries boomerangs that come back to strike him and Truman runs ahead blindly, Dewey becomes the calculating machine, as Truman described him.

Fig. 3.24. *As the Whistle Blows.*
Daniel Fitzpatrick, ink, crayon
and opaque white, 1948. *St.
Louis Post-Dispatch,* SHSM.

Yet another cartoon that depicts
the inauguration of the
campaign. This is not one of
Fitzpatrick's usual thoughtful
efforts.

Fig. 3.25. *Hammering Home a
Campaign Promise.* Walt Kelly,
ink, 1948. *New York Star,* HSTL.

Truman's major criticism of
Taft-Hartley came in the
Cadillac Square speech which
opened his fall campaign. The
above cartoon indirectly alludes
to that address.

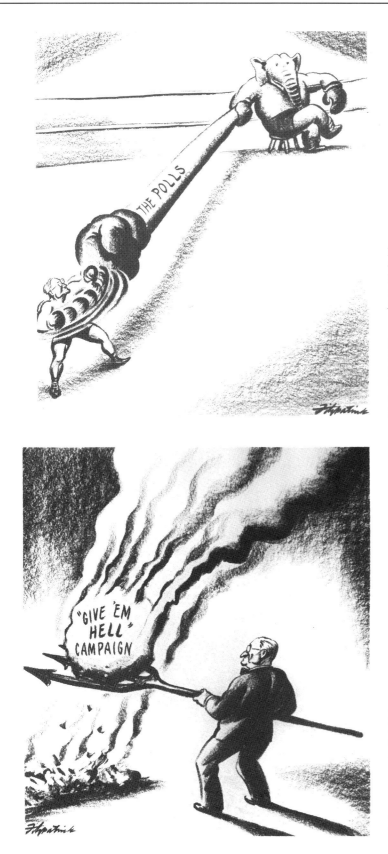

Fig. 3.26. *How to Get That Guard Down?* Daniel Fitzpatrick, ink, crayon, and opaque white, 1948. *St. Louis Post-Dispatch,* SHSM.

In August the Roper poll had Dewey leading Truman, 52.2 percent to 37.2 percent; the October Gallup poll had Dewey ahead, 49.5 percent to 44.5 percent.

Fig. 3.27. *At Basement Level.* Daniel Fitzpatrick, ink, crayon, and opaque white, 1948. *St. Louis Post-Dispatch,* SHSM.

Being in the basement, as Fitzpatrick suggests, reinforced Truman's inclination to run a hard-hitting campaign.

Fig. 3.28. *One Thing in Common*. Leonard D. Warren, ink, crayon, and opaque white, 1948. *Cincinnati Enquirer,* HSTL.

Despite a number of domestic issues that Truman and Dewey used against one another, foreign policy was kept out of the fall campaign. Dewey generally accepted Truman's active foreign policy that assumed United States vital interests were tied to Europe. After the campaign, several Republican leaders chastised Dewey for failing to make Truman's foreign policy a political matter.

Fig. 3.29. (*A Duet.*) Fred L. Packer, ink, crayon, and opaque white, 1948. *Daily Mirror* (New York), HSTL.

Many cartoons of the era frequently focused on government spending and "excessive" taxation. This one rightly implies that Dewey's internationalism and his willingness to accept the New Deal would have meant no appreciable reduction of taxes in his administration.

Fig. 3.30. *Ready or Not —*. Reg Manning, ink and crayon, 1948. *Arizona Republic* (Phoenix), HSTL.

Two days after HST's Dexter speech, Dewey opened his campaign in Des Moines where he spoke in generalities. Two months later he lost Iowa to Truman.

Fig. 3.31. *New Missouri Waltz.* Harold Talburt, crayon, 1948. *Washington Daily News,* HSTL.

HST giving the Eightieth Congress both barrels!

Fig. 3.32. *Gracious — How Uncouth*. Herbert Lawrence Block (Herblock), ink and crayon, 1948. Copyright © Washington Post Co., HSTL.

Dewey's failure to challenge Truman was partly due to the criticism he received in 1944 for his aggressive effort against FDR. A similar approach in 1948 might have aroused sympathy for the underdog Truman, Dewey believed.

Fig. 3.33. *Are Those Trips Necessary?* Frederick O. Seibel, ink (photostatic reproduction), 1948. *Richmond Times-Dispatch*, ALUV.

Seibel suggests that voter apathy characterized this campaign. Of the two, Dewey was much less successful in stirring the voters. His baritone platitudes put people to sleep. Too, he spent much less time on the hustings.

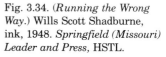

Fig. 3.34. (*Running the Wrong Way*.) Wills Scott Shadburne, ink, 1948. *Springfield (Missouri) Leader and Press*, HSTL.

One of many cartoonists who misinterpreted the way the campaign was going.

Fig. 3.35. *Each to the Other: — Now Look What You've Done*. Jay Norwood (Ding) Darling, ink, 1948. *Des Moines Register* (probably unpublished), UIL.

The cartoon counterpart to the famous *Chicago Tribune* post-election headline! At least Ding left instructions that the drawing should be held until the day after the election. It probably was never printed.

Fig. 3.36. *And on Two Legs.* Karl Kae Knecht, ink and crayon, 1948. *Evansville (Indiana) Courier,* HSTL.

One of several cartoons that emphasizes HST's heroic personal victory.

Fig. 3.37. *You Were So Right, Harry.* Paule Loring, ink and wash, 1948. *Evening Bulletin* (Providence), HSTL.

As few other cartoonists did, Loring admits his misjudgment.

Fig. 3.38. *"Reports of my Political Death . . . "* Bruce Russell, ink, crayon, and collage, 1948. *Los Angeles Herald,* HSTL.

A paraphrasing of Mark Twain seems appropriate!

Fig. 3.39. (*Tipping the Scales.*) Jon Kennedy, ink and crayon, 1948. *Arkansas Democrat,* HSTL.

Cartoonist Jon Kennedy expresses a common theme — HST defying the experts.

Fig. 3.40. (*Teacher's Pet.*)
William (Bill) Mauldin, ink,
1948. United Feature Syndicate,
HSTL.

Voters meted out the greatest
punishment to Henry Wallace
who received no electoral votes;
Thurmond ended up with only
thirty-nine.

Fig. 3.41. *Heaven Protect Him
. . .* Dorman H. Smith, ink and
crayon, c. 1948. NEA Service,
Inc., HSTL.

Everybody loves a winner!

Fig. 3.42. *The One Man Army.*
Jay Norwood (Ding) Darling,
ink, 1948. *Des Moines Register,*
HSTL.

A warm — but untrue —
sentiment. HST had strong
organizational support
particularly from labor.

Fig. 3.43. *No One Was for You
but Me.* Edward Z. (Ned)
Roberts, ink and crayon, 1948.
St. Petersburg Times, HSTL.

Once again, a cartoonist views
HST's victory as a one-man show.

Fig. 3.44. *Guess He Didn't Hear the Umpire.* Jay Norwood (Ding) Darling, ink (photostatic reproduction), 1948. *Des Moines Register,* CLDU.

An excellent caricature but not a suitable analogy. HST didn't win by breaking the rules.

Fig. 3.45. *Who Killed Cock Robin?* Jay Norwood (Ding) Darling, ink (photostatic reproduction), 1948. *Des Moines Register,* CLDU.

Ding in another effort to assess HST's victory, acknowledges organized labor's impact.

Fig. 3.46. *Now the Man's Acquired a Horse.* Bruce Russell, ink, benday film, opaque white, and collage, 1946-48. *Los Angeles Herald,* HSTL.

For the first time since 1946, Truman would have a Democratic Congress to support him as a result of the 1948 election.

4

FAIR DEAL

AT THE BEGINNING of his second term, Harry Truman reached the crest of his presidency. The triumph of 1948 gave him a sense of fulfillment and vindication that few have experienced as president. Liberals finally recognized him as a bona fide leader who embraced the aspirations of the common man. Some labeled him a modern-day Andrew Jackson. Moreover, Truman could now count on a Democratic Congress as a result of the recent election. It was in this spirit that he addressed the American people in January 1949, proclaiming: "Every segment of our population and every individual has a right to expect from our Government a fair deal."

The Fair Deal included the liberal commitments that Truman had espoused in 1948. The Eighty-first, the most active Congress since 1938, made inroads in 1949 when it elevated the minimum wage, extended and increased social security benefits, strengthened farm and conservation programs, and passed the Housing Act, providing for slum clearance and the construction of 810,000 units of low income housing. Even though it failed to move on Truman's most innovative proposals, optimism existed that the second session would produce results.

The Fair Deal did much to encourage economic growth. After a slight recession in 1949, due to Truman's anti-inflation actions, the economy soon responded to government stimuli. By early 1950 wages, prices, profits, and productivity had all increased. The economic pie was enlarged without any redistribution of wealth. Most responsible for the new economic policy was Leon Keyserling, Truman's liberal chairman of the Council of Economic Advisers, who replaced the conservative Edwin Nourse. Keyserling was quite willing to accept a little inflation for economic growth and prosperity. And this indeed was a prosperous time.

Truman's successes in 1949 also included the unification of the military services. This occurred after the departure of Defense Secretary James Forrestal, a longtime obstacle to service integration. His replacement, the broad-shouldered and aggressive Louis Johnson, implemented reforms that HST requested from Congress. As a result, the Department of Defense became a full-fledged executive department. Its secretary now had full authority over the army, navy, and air force, which lost their status as independent executive departments.

On the personal side, the achievements of his daughter made this period increasingly satisfying to Truman. With her father's reluctant approval, the twenty-five-year-old Margaret resumed her professional singing career, begun in 1947, which political events of the following year had interrupted. But in the fall of 1949 Margaret again went on tour, successfully ending it in Washington's Constitution Hall where a packed audience, including a thrilled father, gave her a tremendous ovation. The soprano resumed the tour the following year, closing it once again in Washington on December 5. That day, unknown to Margaret, HST's press secretary and longtime friend Charles Ross died unexpectedly. His death undoubtedly contributed to the president's state of mind the next morning as he turned to the back pages of the *Washington Post* to read music critic Paul Hume's concert evaluation: Margaret "is flat a great deal of the time.... She cannot sing with anything approaching professional finish.... She communicates almost nothing of the music she presents." His criticism angered a loving and protective father who felt compelled to defend the apple of his eye, as he often referred to Margaret. He scrawled the following note to Hume: "I've just read your lousy review.... I've come to the conclusion that you are an 'eight ulcer man on four ulcer pay.' It seems to me that you are a frustrated old man who wishes he could have been successful.... Some day I hope to meet you. When that happens you'll need a new nose, a lot of beefsteak for black eyes, and perhaps a supporter below!"

The president experienced further disappointments in 1950. His difficulties worsened with the Eighty-first Congress. Despite the Dixiecrat party collapse, the southern leadership continually frustrated Truman's Fair Deal proposals. Civil rights legislation had no chance in this Congress. Federal aid to education invited not only the opposition of southern conservatives, but also that of northern Catholics who sought federal aid for private schools. Responding to the American Medical Association's strong campaign against "socialized medicine," Congress ignored Truman's national health insurance proposal. The administration's innovative farm program, the Brannan Plan, met defeat as did HST's efforts to repeal the antilabor Taft-Hartley Act. No doubt the Eighty-first Congress frustrated Truman more than the notorious Eightieth because expectations were so high. But the Eighty-first probably reflected the moderate feelings of the country. While most Americans wished to defend the benefits of the New Deal, they were not anxious to institute additional social welfare legislation. As it turned out, the president significantly popularized ideas that only future Congresses and Americans would accept.

Truman's continued efforts to implement the Fair Deal heightened conservative criticism in late 1950 as had Communist aggression in South Korea, which led to American military involvement. During a period of mounting anti-Communist hysteria, Republicans blamed the administration for failing to prevent the invasion and for sheltering Reds in the federal bureaucracy. These problems not only deflected the president from his domestic program, but they also hindered Democratic candidates in the fall congressional campaign. That election cost the Democrats twenty-eight seats in the House and five in the Senate, many representing leadership positions.

Afterward, two other issues plagued the president's hellish final years. One concerned his seizure of the steel industry in the spring of 1952. The problem began on December 31, 1951, when the union contract expired. The steel workers requested an hourly increase that the administration thought reasonable in light of worker grievances. The administration believed that the steel companies, given their high profit margin, could absorb the wage hike with only a modest increase in steel prices. To do otherwise would aggravate wartime inflation. The steel executives, however, rejected the proposed settlement by asking for increases up to $12 a ton. Consequently, the union announced a strike.

Believing that a national strike would severely hinder the war effort, thus creating a national emergency, Truman employed his inherent constitutional powers as chief executive and commander of the armed forces to take over the steel mills. As most political cartoons suggest, the public thought that Truman had exceeded his powers. Even sympathetic observers believed he created a dangerous precedent that less scrupulous chief executives might someday abuse. By a six to three vote, the U.S. Supreme Court soon ruled the seizure unconstitutional. Seven weeks later, labor and management finally agreed to a compromise settlement. Nonetheless, the steel seizure episode represented a major political defeat for the president.

Truman also had to face the charge of administration corruption. As early as 1949, indications were that his military aide, General Harry Vaughan, was engaged in influence peddling. By 1951 a congressional investigation revealed that federal Reconstruction Finance Corporation officials had lent money for favor. On at least one occasion, the payoff was an $8,000 mink coat. Political cartoonists soon used the mink coat as a symbol of Democratic chicanery. Wrongdoing also existed in the Bureau of Internal Revenue in which high officials accepted bribes to fix tax evasion cases. Misconduct characterized as well the Democratic National Committee whose chairman William Boyle, an old Truman friend, came under fire. Moreover, the Department of Justice, particularly its antitrust and tax division, faced charges of malfeasance. Critics demanded to know why Attorney General J. Howard McGrath had neglected to investigate charges of administration corruption. When an indifferent McGrath failed to cooperate with an independent investigator probing Justice Department activities, the president reluctantly asked McGrath to resign.

Truman himself came under intense criticism even though no one accused him of financial wrongdoing. Detractors nonetheless criticized his choices of appointees, many of whom were cronies or political hacks. They also chided him for defending subordinates who clearly had betrayed his trust. His defense of them created the impression that he condoned their activities. But it is easier to understand HST's actions thirty years later. Truman rightly considered himself a man of high personal integrity and a devoted public servant despite an early loyalty to Boss Pendergast. Consequently, he found it difficult to believe that his own subordinates would be other than honorable men. He had no qualms, then, about returning their loyalty in the face of sometimes exaggerated — if not untrue — press accounts. It is not that HST believed his administration was above reproach, but that the criticism was exaggerated and politically inspired. Nevertheless, enough was revealed to weaken Democratic political fortunes for 1952.

As early as the spring of 1950, Truman had tentatively decided not to seek reelection. As his popularity crumbled, he found little reason to change his mind. He sought instead a strong Democratic nominee who would defend the administration's Fair Deal commitments and foreign policy. Senator Estes Kefauver (Tennessee), the leading Democratic contender in early 1952, was unsatisfactory to Truman. "Cowfever," as HST privately labeled him, had embarrassed the party through his public disclosures of Democratic corruption. Truman thus settled on Adlai Stevenson, the popular and efficient governor of Illinois, who expressed little interest in running.

In personality and outlook, there was a world of difference between the two. Although brilliant and eloquent, Stevenson was indecisive and contemplative. He saw problems in blending tones of gray rather than in absolutes of black and white. Truman rarely recognized such subtlety. No wonder he soon found Stevenson difficult to understand, later referring to him as a "sissy." By convention time the president already had lost some of his enthusiasm for Stevenson, but he nonetheless ensured his nomination to prevent a possible Kefauver victory.

Soon afterward, Stevenson divorced his campaign from the unpopular Truman administration. He established campaign headquarters in Springfield, Illinois, away from Washington, D.C., and the Democratic National Committee. He also replaced the Truman-appointed national committee chairman without first informing the president. More disturbing, Stevenson acknowledged that a "mess" existed in Washington. Not only did he seem to be running against Truman as well as Eisenhower, the Republican nominee, but he also failed to give the Republicans "hell."

After repeated Republican attacks on his administration, Truman entered the campaign. He did so as much to defend his record as he did to seek a Stevenson victory. Reminiscent of 1948, Truman whistle-stopped across the country, labeling Ike a hypocrite and a "stooge for Wall Street," among other things. But HST's fireworks failed to duplicate the Democratic victory of 1948. The big difference was that the extremely popular Eisenhower had replaced Dewey. Moreover, the aging Truman administration was more vulnerable, particularly in its foreign policy as the three-year-old Korean War lingered on without resolution.

Fig. 4.1. *The New Truman.*
Frederick O. Seibel, ink, 1949.
Richmond Times-Dispatch,
ALUV.

No greater feeling can come to
an "accidental" president. This
fact perhaps partly explains
HST's intense campaign of 1948
and also the efforts of Theodore
Roosevelt (1904), Lyndon
Johnson (1964), and other
"accidental" presidents.

Fig. 4.2. *The New Look.* Daniel
Fitzpatrick, ink, crayon, and
opaque white, 1949. *St. Louis
Post-Dispatch,* SHSM.

A rejuvenated president
illuminates the newly elected
Democratic Congress.

Fig. 4.3. *When Washington Moves to Kansas City.* Silvey Jackson Ray, ink, c. 1949. *Kansas City Star,* HSTL.

Occasionally, along with administration officials, HST returned to his Kansas City bailiwick as he did in the fall of 1949 to deliver a speech.

Fig. 4.4. *Tin Horns Are Drowned Out!* John Baer, ink, 1950. *Labor,* HSTL.

A favorable view of the Truman administration's economic policy. The opposition of Republican Senators Joseph McCarthy (Wisconsin) and Taft (Ohio) went virtually unheard.

Fig. 4.5. *Alexander's Ragtime Band.* Daniel Dowling, ink, 1949. *New York Herald-Tribune,* HSTL.

In October 1949 the orthodox Edwin Nourse resigned as chairman of the Council of Economic Advisers because of Truman's antirecession policies that included deficit spending.

Fig. 4.6. *Everybody Hang on Back in the Trailer.* Daniel Dowling, ink and benday film, 1950. *New York Herald-Tribune,* HSTL.

This cartoon indicates that by 1950 the liberal Leon Keyserling was in the driver's seat regarding the administration's economic policy.

Fig. 4.7. *Let Us Pray.*
Czermanski, ink and watercolor
(photostatic reproduction), 1949.
Fortune, HSTL..

With an armed Defense
Secretary Louis Johnson
standing behind the president,
HST performs the "shotgun"
ceremony, merging the three
military services. Second from
the right is General Omar
Bradley, the army chief of staff,
who became the first chairman
of the joint chiefs of staff.

Fig. 4.8. (*A Partisan Aria.*) Bill
Dyer, ink and crayon, 1949.
Knoxville News-Sentinel, HSTL.

During Margaret Truman's 1949
concert tour, at least one
cartoonist could not resist a
political comment. It underscores
the difficulty of being a
presidential offspring.

Fig. 4.9. *If Margaret Gets Any More Popular.* Vaughn Shoemaker, ink, benday film, and opaque white, c. 1950. *New York Herald-Tribune,* HSTL.

This cartoon acknowledges Margaret's popularity. But it would not have bothered HST to be referred to as Margaret's father.

Fig. 4.10. *Not So Silent Knight.* Bert Whitman, ink and crayon, 1950. *Stockton (California) Record,* HSTL.

As did most political cartoonists, Whitman criticizes HST's "spasm" to Paul Hume, the *Washington Post* music critic.

Fig. 4.11. *Harry S. Truman —
Doctor of Letters.* Eldon L.
Pletcher, ink and crayon
(clipping from the *Sioux City
Journal*), 1950.

As Pletcher suggests, Truman's
impulsive note to Hume was not
the only scorching missive he
wrote. Many of them, however,
were not sent. After he vented his
anger, he merely filed the letter.

Fig. 4.12. *An Old Neighbor
Stops By.* Hal Coffman, ink and
crayon, c. 1949. *Ft. Worth
Star-Telegram,* HSTL.

The Dixiecrats returned to the
Democratic party after 1948.
There was nowhere else to go. In
fact, despite frequent differences
with the national Democratic
party, southerners remained
Democratic until many defected
to Barry Goldwater in 1964.

Fig. 4.13. *Aw — C'mon, Mule, — Drink!* Bill McClanahan, ink and crayon, c. 1949. *Dallas Morning News,* HSTL.

The mulish southern Democrats were a major obstacle to Truman's Fair Deal program. They joined with Republicans to vote down several of HST's key reform bills.

Fig. 4.14. (*He Forgot That Mules Can Balk, Too.*) Ned White, ink, crayon, and opaque white, 1949. *Akron Beacon Journal,* HSTL.

This cartoon is a little misleading. Republicans were not always laughing in 1949. The Eighty-first Congress cooperated on several Fair Deal proposals.

Fig. 4.15. *The Honeymoon Is Over.* Fred L. Packer, ink, crayon, and opaque white, c. 1949. *Daily Mirror* (New York), HSTL.

An unflattering caricature of the difficulties Truman faced with the Eighty-first Congress.

Fig. 4.16. *Ol' Mac Truman Had a Farm, Ee-I-Ee-I-Ouch.* Gib Crockett, ink, benday film, and opaque white, 1949. *Washington Star,* HSTL.

Crockett sympathetically portrays Truman's frustration by late 1949.

Fig. 4.17. *Last Year's Nest — With a Few Additions.* Edward Kuekes, ink, 1950. *Plain Dealer* (Cleveland), HSTL.

In his 1950 State of the Union address, Truman again called for the enactment of pending Fair Deal programs, including national health insurance and Point Four, a technical assistance program for "underdeveloped areas." The Brannan Plan, a novel farm assistance program benefiting consumers through lower farm prices, was a new proposal. None of these programs made it through the Congress.

Fig. 4.18. *Shotgun Wedding.* Ross Lewis, ink and crayon, 1949. *Milwaukee Journal,* HSTL.

Cartoonist Lewis rightly contends that political pressure wedded HST to Taft-Hartley repeal. If organized labor were not as opposed, Truman would have likely favored amending the law.

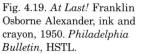

Fig. 4.19. *At Last!* Franklin Osborne Alexander, ink and crayon, 1950. *Philadelphia Bulletin,* HSTL.

As this 1950 cartoon reveals, HST occasionally invoked the Taft-Hartley Law to prevent labor stoppages. In 1948 alone Truman used it seven times.

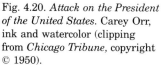

Fig. 4.20. *Attack on the President of the United States.* Carey Orr, ink and watercolor (clipping from *Chicago Tribune,* copyright © 1950).

By 1950 public criticism of Truman increased. The Orr cartoon is one of the more vicious examples.

Fig. 4.21. *"Tell Me, Alben . . . "* James Berryman, ink and benday film (photostatic reproduction), 1950. *Washington Star,* HSTL.

Because of the Korean War, Truman did not campaign in the 1950 Congressional election. Thus much of the burden fell upon Vice-President Alben Barkley who cannot be blamed for "GOP gains." Actually, in an off-year election, the loss of twenty-eight House and five Senate seats for an incumbent party was not unusual. Much more disturbing was the defeat of Scott Lucas (Illinois), the Senate majority leader; Francis Myers (Pennsylvania), the Senate majority whip; and such respected Senators as Millard Tydings (Maryland).

Fig. 4.22. *"Of Course I'm Not Giving Up . . . "* James Berryman, ink and benday film, 1951. *Washington Star,* HSTL.

By 1951 the Korean War prolongation meant a shifting of priorities, as Berryman concedes. In fact, the administration increased the national defense budget from $17.7 billion in 1950 to $53.4 billion for 1951.

Fig. 4.23. *Maybe I Was Better Off When I Wasn't Invited.* Herbert Lawrence Block (Herblock), ink, crayon, and opaque white, 1951. Copyright © Washington Post Co., HSTL.

War mobilization meant tax increases. That, to Truman, was a more satisfactory solution than government borrowing to finance the war. More so than FDR, he wanted to place the financial burden upon his own rather than on future generations. By 1951, with Republican support, HST managed to get three large tax bills through the Congress. Even so, the national debt increased appreciably during the war years.

Fig. 4.24. *We're Waiting to Hear from the Principal.* Silvey Jackson Ray, ink, crayon, and opaque white, 1952. *Kansas City Star,* SHSM.

During wartime, past presidents often extended their authority immensely. The justification was that the war emergency necessitated such broad executive action. In some instances, the U.S. Supreme Court approved. In Truman's case the Court contended that his seizure, coming without statutory authority, represented an unconstitutional usurpation of legislative power.

Fig. 4.25. *Balance of Power.* Burris Jenkins, ink, crayon, and opaque white, 1952. *New York Journal-American,* HSTL.

Another critical cartoon contending that HST had exceeded the Constitution in the steel seizure case.

Fig. 4.26. *Still Bucking the Tide.* Herc Ficklen, ink, crayon, and opaque white, 1952. *Dallas Morning News,* HSTL.

Truman's liberal view of the "inherent powers" of the presidency left him "high and dry." Critics felt that the president need not have depended on such authority, for his invoking of the Taft-Hartley Act could have delayed the strike eighty days.

Fig. 4.27. *On Different Pages in History.* Don Hesse, ink, graphite, crayon, and opaque white, 1952. *St. Louis Globe-Democrat,* SHSM.

A typical example of an editorial cartoonist who employed the mink coat symbol to publicize Democratic corruption. Hesse, drawing for the conservative *St. Louis Globe Democrat,* comes down hard on HST.

Fig. 4.28. *Look Out Harry, Here Comes a Library.* Daniel Fitzpatrick, ink and crayon, 1951. *St. Louis Post-Dispatch,* SHSM.

Along with the mink coat, Fitzpatrick publicizes other symbols of Democratic wrongdoing. A "five percenter" was an influence peddler who, after using his political connections to secure a government contract for a client, received a five percent kickback. Sometimes other gifts such as deep freezers were exchanged for favors.

Fig. 4.29. *Boyle on the Neck.* Don Hesse, ink, graphite, and crayon, 1951. *St. Louis Globe-Democrat,* SHSM.

Democratic National Chairman William Boyle, a longtime Truman friend, caused HST's neck "boil." The *St. Louis Globe-Democrat* exposed Boyle for misusing his office for political and personal financial considerations.

Fig. 4.30. *"What's a Republican Doing with Influence?"* James Berryman, ink and benday film, c. 1951. *Washington Star,* HSTL.

Republican National Chairman Guy Gabrielson also was exposed as an influence peddler following a Senate subcommittee investigation.

Fig. 4.31. *One Coat Won't Cover That — Harry.* Don Hesse, ink, crayon, and opaque white, 1951. *St. Louis Globe-Democrat,* SHSM.

HST did not mollify critics by obtaining the resignations of a few culpable staffers in the Bureau of Internal Revenue and in other federal agencies.

Fig. 4.32. *"Why Didn't You Tell Me . . . ?"* James Berryman, ink and crayon (photostatic reproduction), 1951. *Washington Star,* HSTL.

Assistant Attorney General Theron Lamar Caudle, head of the Justice Department's tax division, was forced to resign after a congressional subcomittee exposed Caudle's conflicts of interest and his related failure to prosecute tax evasion cases. Apparently, Joe Short, HST's press secretary, initially misled the president about Caudle.

Fig. 4.33. *No, Your Majesty, Not Every Day.* Robbie Robinson, ink, crayon, and opaque white, 1951. *Indianapolis News,* HSTL.

On the day HST fired Attorney General McGrath, he met with Queen Juliana of the Netherlands.

Fig. 4.34. (*Can't Cover Up the Smell.*) Karl Kae Knecht, ink and crayon, 1952. *Evansville (Indiana) Courier,* HSTL.

HST's 1952 State of the Union reeked of scandals, according to Knecht.

Fig. 4.35. (*Trying to Make Up His Mind.*) Karl Kae Knecht, ink and crayon, 1952. *The Evansville (Indiana) Courier,* HSTL.

Beginning in 1946, President Truman escaped some of the presidential pressures by vacationing in Key West, Florida. In the winter of 1952, he again went South.

Fig. 4.36. (*The Capitol Is Fogged In.*) Cyrus Hungerford, ink, c. 1952. *Pittsburgh Post-Gazette,* AWC.

As Washington's political climate worsened, Truman found Key West even more of a haven. It was sometimes difficult returning to reality.

Fig. 4.37. *Invitation to Snowballs*. Reg Manning, ink and crayon, 1952. *Arizona Republic* (Phoenix), HSTL.

Primarily because of projected defense expenditures, the proposed budget for 1953 represented a substantial increase over 1952 expenditures.

Fig. 4.38. *The Enigma*. Edward Kuekes, ink, 1951. *Plain Dealer* (Cleveland), HSTL.

Although HST had privately decided not to seek reelection, he kept the public guessing until March 29, 1952. Prospective Democratic candidates were in a quandary until then.

Fig. 4.39. *Well! — Is You or Ain't You?* Silvey Jackson Ray, ink and crayon, 1952. *Kansas City Star,* SHSM.

Another cartoon showing Truman's enigmatic silence. In early March he momentarily reassessed his position about not running since at that time Stevenson expressed little interest in the presidency. The front-running Kefauver was unacceptable to HST.

Fig. 4.40. *Not Selling Anything, This Time.* Reg Manning, ink, crayon, and opaque white, 1952. *Arizona Republic* (Phoenix), HSTL.

In January Kefauver visited HST to discuss his possible candidacy. The president was polite but noncommittal.

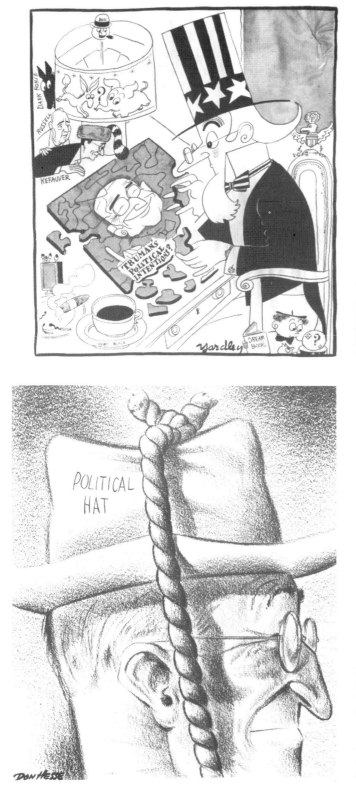

Fig. 4.41. (*A Real Puzzle*.) Richard Yardley, ink and benday film, c. 1952. *Sun* (Baltimore), SHSM.

Yardley's amusing drawing suggests yet another presidential prospect, Senator Richard Russell (Georgia). In 1952 a southerner had virtually no chance of capturing the party nomination.

Fig. 4.42. *Draft Proof Now.* Don Hesse, ink, crayon, and opaque white, 1952. *St. Louis Globe-Democrat,* SHSM.

Truman's statement of March 29 unequivocally removed him from consideration.

Fig. 4.43. *No Encore.* John Collins, ink, 1952. *Gazette* (Montreal), HSTL.

Collins reveals a somber HST immediately following his 1952 withdrawal.

Fig. 4.44. *Tum De Dum, Ta Da, Ta La —.* Herbert Lawrence Block (Herblock), ink, crayon and opaque white, 1952. Copyright © Washington Post Co., HSTL.

Herblock portrays a buoyant Truman intent on traveling after his presidency.

Fig. 4.45. *Missouri's Dark Horse.* Daniel Fitzpatrick, ink, crayon, and opaque white, 1952. *St. Louis Post-Dispatch,* SHSM.

HST also entertained some thought about returning to Washington, D.C., as a United States Senator. Bess Truman vetoed this possibility, however.

Fig. 4.46. *The Voice of Experience.* Newton Pratt, ink, crayon, and opaque white, 1952. McClatchy Newspapers, HSTL.

HST warns Senator Taft, a leading candidate for the GOP nomination, to beware of the aspiring General Douglas MacArthur.

Fig. 4.47. *"I'm Betting That Ike Can't Ride 'Im!"* James Berryman, ink and benday film, 1952. *Washington Star,* HSTL.

In mid-May HST delivered a spirited attack against the Republican conservatives. Most political commentators considered Ike a moderate, if not a liberal, Republican. Note Berryman's inscription!

Fig. 4.48. *Well, It's Leap Year.* Silvey Jackson Ray, ink, 1952. *Kansas City Star,* SHSM.

On the eve of the Democratic National Convention, the Democratic swing is clearly to the reluctant Stevenson. Meanwhile, Kefauver's gestures receive no attention. A seemingly detached HST views the activity from afar. At this point, the president was disillusioned with Adlai.

Fig. 4.49. *Mr. Delegate at Large.* Daniel Fitzpatrick, ink, crayon, and opaque white, 1952. *St. Louis Post-Dispatch,* SHSM.

Although HST was selected a Missouri delegate-at-large to the Democratic convention, his alternate, Thomas J. Gavin of Kansas City, sat for him as the president remained in Washington, D.C., until the last day of the convention.

Fig. 4.50. *Get Me Springfield.* Don Hesse, graphite and opaque white, 1952. *St. Louis Globe-Democrat,* SHSM.

Truman's call to the Stevenson headquarters followed the latter's "mess in Washington" remark.

Fig. 4.51. *"I'm Telling You Adlai
. . ."* Gib Crockett, ink and
benday film, 1952. *Washington
Star,* HSTL.

HST advises Stevenson that he
could not criticize a Democratic
Congress. Nor, by implication,
should he speak disparagingly of
the Democratic administration.

Fig. 4.52. *Papoose.* Don Hesse,
graphite, crayon, and opaque
white, 1952. *St. Louis
Globe-Democrat,* SHSM.

This cartoon is misleading. Even
though Truman embarked on a
whistle-stop campaign as
strenuous as that of 1948, he
could not carry or control
Stevenson. The latter followed a
strategy and philosophy that
HST did not always approve.

Fig. 4.53. *Terrible Tempered Swan Song.* Don Hesse, graphite, crayon, and opaque white, 1952. *St. Louis Globe-Democrat,* SHSM.

The postelection cartoon came just before Ike's meeting with the anti-Truman MacArthur. The latter professed a solution to end the Korean War. Truman angrily suggested that if the general had such a plan, he should present it to the proper authorities for action.

Fig. 4.54. *Truman Press Conference.* Daniel Dowling, ink and benday film, 1952. *New York Herald-Tribune,* LC.

HST's press conferences often provided such fireworks. The president responded swiftly and openly to reporters' questions. In his last press conference, he not only belittled MacArthur's proposed Korean solution, but he also jumped on President-elect Eisenhower's announced trip to Korea. That announcement, Truman said, "was a piece of demagoguery."

5

COLD WAR

IN 1947 an eminent American journalist called the emerging United States-Soviet conflict a Cold War. That characterization succinctly captured the ideological, diplomatic, and economic warfare associated with East-West relations. Different ideologies, national security goals, and economic objectives brought on the Cold War. It rapidly became President Truman's greatest challenge as Soviet expansion threatened non-Communist governments in Eastern Europe. American policy-makers soon believed that unless the United States boldly responded, the Soviet Union would engulf most of Europe, if not the world. Consequently, President Truman gave foreign policy his primary attention. Historians evaluate his presidency accordingly. Most give him high marks for a foreign policy that saved Western Europe both politically and economically. Despite some setbacks, his bold actions elsewhere were also instrumental in arresting Communist aggression.

At the beginning of Truman's presidency, allied forces had already initiated the final assault against Nazi Germany. The termination of the European war seemed only a matter of months away. In the Far East Japan's resistance, although still formidable, was crumbling. Yet, as Truman would soon learn, the ending of hostilities would not automatically ensure peace and harmony. For example, differences existed among the allied powers over how national security could best be assured in the postwar period. Among the major powers, the United States made the greatest commitment to collective security through a United Nations organization. The USSR's Joseph Stalin and Great Britain's Winston Churchill placed more faith on spheres of influence and favorable balances of power, respectively. Thus, on the verge of victory, the Grand Alliance showed signs of coming apart.

Truman faced these monumental problems without any experience in foreign policy. His senatorial career had centered on domestic matters. As vice-president, his contact with President Roosevelt had been minimal. Given such handicaps, it is amazing that he performed so well.

In 1945 HST's inexperience, occasional self-doubt, and the changing world situation led to a fluctuating approach. His first move was to proceed with the UN organizational meeting in San Francisco that April in order to draft a charter. Soviet Foreign Minister V. M. Molotov visited the president in the White House before attending the conference. It was here that Truman first charged the Soviets with imposing a Communist system upon Poland and Rumania. Molotov, taken aback by Truman's stance and tone, responded: "I have never been talked to like that in my life." Truman supposedly retorted, "Carry out your agreements and you won't get talked to like that."

The conflict over Eastern Europe — particularly Poland — ignited the Cold War. Soviet "bad faith" had a tremendous influence on Truman especially after Soviet control tightened and eventually spread to Hungary and Czechoslovakia by 1948. To Truman the Soviet Union had become a "world bully" that would more likely cooperate if the United States were firm. The Soviets, meanwhile, thought Truman "unfriendly." Stalin soon complained of American insensitivity to Soviet security considerations. Soviet influence in border countries such as Poland was necessary, according to Stalin, because invaders had too often gained access across the flat Polish plain. In World War II nearly 20 million Russians died and over 30,000 Soviet industrial plants and 40,000 miles of railroad track were destroyed. "Things are not bad in the United States," Stalin said, as if to underscore differences in wartime losses. Moreover, Stalin resented the double standard he thought Western allies applied to Soviet security interests. While they objected to Soviet influences in Poland, the French and British retained forces from the Suez to Indochina in an effort to bolster colonial empires. Stalin accepted British activity in Greece and Belgium, he maintained, because he knew how important these countries were to British security. He could not understand why he failed to receive the same consideration.

HST perhaps realized the conflict was more complex and dangerous than he originally thought. He therefore adopted a more conciliatory tack toward the Soviet Union by mid-May 1945. He sent FDR's most trusted adviser, Harry Hopkins, to Moscow to resolve differences. There was no American leader whom Stalin liked better. Hopkins managed to secure some concessions that eased the Polish controversy temporarily. Truman personally attended the Potsdam Conference, the first Big-Three conference since FDR's death. The mid-July assemblage near Berlin was Truman's only meeting with Stalin. In later years, HST claimed that he "liked that little son of a bitch" and even compared him to Tom Pendergast. The fact is that the lengthy, frustrating sessions failed to resolve differences over Eastern Europe and on other matters.

While at Potsdam, Truman learned of the successful testing of the atomic bomb, which proved more destructive than expected. It quickly affected United States-Soviet relations. It meant that the United States no longer had to depend on Russian military participation against Japan, lessening the need for Western-Soviet cooperation. Moreover, with such colossal power, American leaders believed the United States could alter events in Eastern Europe. Political cartoonists frequently portrayed the bomb's presence at the negotiation table. Far from making the Soviet Union "more manageable," as Secretary of State Jimmy Byrnes predicted, the bomb increased the Soviet Union's resistance and determination to create her own arsenal. If anything, the bomb heightened mutual distrust and fear, a prevailing characteristic of the emerging Cold War.

The Soviet Union also failed to react favorably to economic leverage despite American economic influence that was indeed formidable. In 1945 the Truman administration made it possible for Moscow to obtain a $1 billion reconstruction loan provided that the latter adhered to United States objectives in Eastern Europe. The Soviet Union instead sought rehabilitation through reparations and war booty from East Germany and Eastern Europe, further weakening Soviet-American relations.

The Cold War worsened in 1946. Attempts to internationalize the atomic bomb through a UN Atomic Energy Commission failed. Too, the Soviet Union refused to withdraw her troops from northern Iran as promised. Russia probably sought a northern Iranian protectorate, causing a United States protest in the UN. At this time Truman privately exclaimed: "I'm tired [of] babying the Soviets." He ordered Secretary of State Byrnes to make no more concessions.

By 1947 the emerging Cold War led to the development of

the United States containment policy. Designed by State Department officials, it remained HST's basic approach for the duration of his presidency. Containment committed the United States to employing economic, political, or military force, wherever necessary, to contain Soviet expansion. Its first application came after the British government revealed to the United States that it could no longer provide economic and military assistance to Greece and Turkey. The Truman administration believed that these countries were in danger of Soviet domination. The Russians had already pressured the Turks regarding the Dardanelles Strait; civil war raged in Greece between an autocratic, British-backed government and a coalition of Communist and liberal rebels.

In March HST went before a joint session of Congress, requesting $400 million for economic and military aid to Greece and Turkey. He also stated, in what was soon called the Truman Doctrine, that "it must be the policy of the United States to support free peoples who are resisting attempted subjugation by armed minorities or by outside pressures." Undersecretary of State Dean Acheson had already informed congressional leaders that the real threat was Soviet Communism that sought control over Europe, the Middle East, South Asia, and Africa. The parsimonious but alarmed Republican Congress funded the appropriation, and the Truman Doctrine contributed to the quelling of the Greek revolution.

A logical extension of Greek-Turkish aid was the Marshall Plan, an economic assistance program for Western and Central Europe. Named after HST's secretary of state, George Marshall, the idea was first proposed in June 1947. At that time starvation conditions existed throughout much of Europe, and a terrible inflation swept France and West Germany. Moreover, economic prostration jeopardized American trade and prosperity. The Truman administration hoped by initiating economic revitalization that it would also prevent Soviet expansion in countries such as France and Italy where the Communist party already had considerable influence.

For the next five years, Marshall Plan assistance proved crucial to the economic recovery of Western Europe. Some seventeen nations profited from the $13 billion transfusion. As a result, by 1950 Western Europe was exceeding its prewar production by 25 percent. American economic interests also benefited, while the Communist threat in Italy and France receded. The Soviet Union, however, tightened its hold on

Eastern Europe in response to the American aid program.

By 1948 Cold War differences sharpened. After the Communist coup in Czechoslovakia, Truman accepted an invitation of Western European countries to join a defensive pact. In June the president secured the endorsement of the United States Senate, paving the way the following year for United States entry into the North Atlantic Treaty Organization (NATO) in which eleven signatories committed themselves to each other's defense. For the first time since 1800, when it terminated the French alliance, the United States joined a formal military alliance.

In this same period the United States clashed with the Soviet Union over Berlin. In June 1948 the Russians closed all surface traffic into West Berlin, located 100 miles within the Soviet zone of East Germany. The allies had occupation rights there but the Western right of access was never put into writing. Consequently, at a time when allied cooperation was breaking down in Germany and when it appeared that the West would establish a separate West German state, the Soviets sought to expel the Western powers from West Berlin.

As in other crises, the Truman administration responded immediately and imaginatively. Its objective was to preserve Western interests in West Berlin. To do otherwise would have weakened West German confidence in American resolve and undermined the emerging Western alliance. Yet Truman stopped short of employing American troops, which might have led to war. Instead, the United States and Great Britain airlifted supplies to the West Berliners. The airlift, another manifestation of Truman's containment policy, lasted for 324 days and ultimately delivered 13,000 tons of goods daily. The West Berliners soon ate better than they had prior to the blockade. By May 1949 the Soviet Union ended the blockade. After all, it had only succeeded in trumpeting American ingenuity and solidifying Western unity.

In September 1949 the Soviet Union challenged that strength by exploding their atomic bomb, causing Truman to accelerate the hydrogen bomb project. In addition, he bolstered NATO by sending additional combat divisions to West Germany. He also pushed for West German rearmament, but because of French and British opposition, West Germany remained unarmed until 1955.

The Truman administration had concentrated much of its foreign policy in Europe where it believed United States vital interests lay. In Asia, China represented America's initial concern. But by 1949 Chiang Kai-shek's Nationalist government had squandered American military and economic assistance totaling nearly $3 billion, enabling the Communists to control China. Short of military intervention, there was little Truman could do to save Chiang's corrupt and inept regime. Yet critics persisted in blaming the Truman administration for the "loss" of China. Some even charged that Communist sympathizers in the State Department were responsible for the "sell out."

The Korean War eventually increased the political vulnerability of Truman's foreign policy. By 1948 the Korean peninsula, which bordered Manchurian China, had been divided at the thirty-eighth parallel after the United States and the Soviet Union failed to agree on a united Korean government. On June 25, 1950, the Communist North Koreans attacked South Korea. Truman officials assumed — perhaps wrongly — that the Soviet Union engineered that invasion. If it had succeeded, Truman believed, the Soviets would have extended their aggression in Asia and then swallowed up the Near East and Europe. He invoked the "lessons" of the immediate past in arguing that the United Nations must not fail as the League of Nations had done in response to the 1931 Japanese invasion of Manchuria.

One day after the North Korean attack, an American resolution in the Security Council branded the North Koreans as aggressors. On June 27 Truman ordered air and naval units into action. That same day, the UN recommended that member nations provide military assistance to South Korea. Sixteen nations eventually contributed to the UN "police action," with the United States providing most of the forces and ultimately suffering 142,000 casualties.

Under the direction of General Douglas MacArthur, UN Supreme Commander, the United States-directed operation pushed the North Koreans back to the thirty-eighth parallel by September. Later that month, the Truman administration's objectives changed from containment to liberation. In early October, the UN endorsed Truman's decision to move troops into North Korea. At a Wake Island meeting that same month, General MacArthur assured the president that the war would be over by Thanksgiving.

MacArthur had discounted the intervention of China despite that country's repeated warnings as UN forces moved closer to the border. China's intervention in November eventually forced UN forces back into South Korea, causing Truman to seek a political solution. This placed HST in conflict with MacArthur who remained committed to Korean liberation. The president refused to escalate the war because it would cost this country dearly in manpower and weaken the American commitment to Europe where United States' vital interests lay. MacArthur's public criticism challenged the president's role as chief spokesman of American foreign policy. Truman had no alternative but to dismiss him.

The firing of MacArthur caused public opinion to turn sharply against the Truman administration. Initially, strongly in support of Truman's decisive action against the North Korean attack, public sentiment began to shift after the Chinese intervention. The military reversals frustrated Americans who believed in United States omnipotence. Many failed to accept or understand the return to containment in Korea. Moreover, when peace negotiations produced no settlement, frustration and criticism increased.

Given these misconceptions it is easier to understand, then, why many Americans readily accepted Senator Joseph McCarthy's charges that Red sympathizers in the State Department prevented a military victory in Korea. In 1952 many Americans took McCarthy seriously, for they feared the domestic dangers of Communism that supposedly threatened the very fabric of our society. "McCarthyism," as Herblock termed it, actually preceded McCarthy's barrages. It had gathered momentum during the early Cold War as Americans first experienced that frustrating mode of warfare. By 1947 Truman administration officials might have contributed to domestic anxieties by exaggerating the Soviet menace abroad so as to secure congressional and public support for their foreign policy initiatives.

Critics soon put HST on the defensive by charging that the administration did nothing to eradicate Communists from the federal agencies. In 1947 HST thus began the systematic investigation of all federal employees. This led to the dismissal or resignation of over 2,000 employees amid liberal criticism that civil liberties had been compromised. Despite the loyalty probe, HST still faced Republican censure particularly after congressional committee testimony charged that Alger Hiss, a noted New Dealer and State Department official, had been a Communist in the 1930s. Hiss's subsequent conviction and the continuing implication that there were other spies in government put the Truman administration further on the defensive by 1950. By then the administration was indeed vulnerable to McCarthy's brash and unsubstantiated charges. Its failure to produce "victory" in Korea only strengthened the McCarthyites and contributed to Eisenhower's 1952 victory.

Fig. 5.1. " . . . *We Are Going to Win the Peace, Too.*" Clifford Kennedy Berryman, ink (clipping from *Washington Post*), 1945.

In 1945 American power and optimism were evident. As in 1918, Americans were determined to shape the postwar peace.

Fig. 5.2. " . . . *How Long Will It Take the Senate to Ratify It?*" James Berryman, ink, 1945. *Washington Star,* LC.

Because of emerging Cold War differences, it took the delegates in San Francisco eight weeks to draw up a United Nations charter. Republican Senator Arthur Vandenburg (Michigan) played a key role as an American delegate. Democratic Senator Tom Connally (Texas), as chairman of the Senate Foreign Relations Committee, was expected to play a leading part in obtaining Senate approval of the charter.

Fig. 5.3. *"Mr. President, Please Wire Hopkins to Be Careful . . ."* James Berryman, ink, 1945. *Washington Evening Star,* HSTL.

In late 1945 HST sent Harry Hopkins to Moscow to improve relations. Hopkins had a special relationship with the Soviets dating back to the early war years. Secretary of State Edward Stettinius questioned whether Hopkins had carried that friendship too far.

Fig. 5.4. *His Credit's Okay, but That Stuff Is Rationed.* Calvin Lane Alley, ink, 1945. *Nashville Banner,* HSTL.

At the February Yalta Conference, FDR had supported Stalin's Far East objectives, some at Japan's expense, in exchange for Soviet military involvement against Japan ninety days after the war in Europe ended. In mid-July Truman reminded Stalin of that understanding.

Fig. 5.5. " . . . *I'm from Missouri.*" Karl Kae Knecht, ink (photographic reproduction), 1945. *Evansville (Indiana) Courier,* HSTL.

The well-publicized Potsdam Conference spawned considerable cartoonist attention. This drawing depicts the three main participants at the convening of the conference on July 17. Besides HST, Premiers Winston Churchill and Joseph Stalin represented the other two powers.

Fig. 5.6. (*Will There Be Yet Another Replacement?*) Karl Kae Knecht, ink, 1945. *Evansville (Indiana) Courier,* HSTL.

In the midst of the Potsdam Conference, the British voters rejected Churchill's Conservative government. The main issues in that election had little to do with foreign policy. The Labour party leader, Clement R. Attlee, replaced Churchill as prime minister.

Fig. 5.7. (*Like Pennies from Heaven.*) Karl Kae Knecht, ink, 1945. *Evansville (Indiana) Courier,* HSTL.

The United States Senate overwhelmingly approved the UN charter at the time of Potsdam. That action, along with the settlement at Potsdam of the German reparation and other related issues, created some reason for hope despite unresolved problems.

Fig. 5.8. (*Turning Off the Hydrant.*) Clifford Kennedy Berryman, ink (clipping from *New York Times*), 1945.

Following V-E Day in 1945, HST began to terminate Lend-Lease. Reflecting the feelings of the Senate, he resisted using that assistance program for postwar reconstruction. In May the administration had so suddenly ended aid to the Soviet Union that Stalin angrily interpreted it as economic pressure. Soviet-American relations became even more strained.

Fig. 5.9. "... *Solve This One Real Quick!*" Clifford Kennedy Berryman, ink (clipping from *Washington Star*), 1945.

HST found out about the bomb shortly after becoming president. The above cartoon came out two days after the bomb was dropped on Hiroshima on August 6. The person next to Truman is Henry Stimson, secretary of war, who first informed him of that "terrible weapon."

Fig. 5.10. *Good Trick If We Can Do It.* James Berryman, ink (clipping from *Washington Star*), 1945.

For awhile the Truman administration attempted to internationalize control of atomic weaponry through the United Nations. No acceptable plan emerged that satisfied the United States and the Soviets. Three years later, the Russians tested their first atomic bomb.

Fig. 5.11. *"How Many Lives
. . . ?"* Clifford Kennedy
Berryman, ink, 1947.
Washington Evening Star, HSTL.

The United Nations organization
quickly reflected Cold War
differences with the Soviet
Union often exercising the veto
power in the Security Council.

Fig. 5.12. *Hi-Yah Pal.* Jay
Norwood (Ding) Darling, ink,
1947. *Des Moines Register,* UIL.

The Republican Ding forces a
comparison between HST's and
Stalin's veto actions.

Fig. 5.13. *"General, This Is Quite a Shock . . . "* James Berryman, ink, c. 1946. *Washington Star,* HSTL.

The meeting probably took place in 1946 when HST appointed General Eisenhower chief of staff at a White House meeting. During this period, the Truman-Eisenhower relationship was one of mutual respect.

Fig. 5.14. *With The Rest of the World As It Is.* Vaughn Shoemaker, ink and crayon, 1947. *Chicago Daily News,* SHSM.

The Cold War made the United States appreciate her neighbors more. In 1947 HST even undertook a good will trip to Mexico City.

Fig. 5.15. *"Can't You Fellows Spare a Little Something . . . ?"* Clifford Kennedy Berryman, ink (clipping from *Washington Evening Star*), 1947.

In 1947 Henry Wallace remained a critic of the Truman foreign policy. While favoring economic assistance, he opposed United States military aid to Greece and Turkey, labeling the Truman Doctrine "a military lend-lease program." Wallace also favored rehabilitation loans to the Soviet Union to improve political and economic relations.

Fig. 5.16. *Another Man O'war?* Daniel Holland, ink (clipping from *Washington Times-Herald*, copyright © the *Chicago Tribune*, 1947).

Holland, of the isolationist and conservative *Chicago Tribune*, impugns Truman's motives in coming to the aid of the Greek state.

Fig. 5.17. *An Unlucky Day for the Traffic Cop.* Cyrus Hungerford, ink, 1947. *Pittsburgh Post-Gazette,* AWC.

As Hungerford suggests, the Truman Doctrine did not prevent Soviet consolidation of its sphere in Eastern Europe. Nevertheless, it prevented a Communist government in Greece, and in conjunction with the Marshall Plan, it undercut Communist activity in Western and Southern Europe.

Fig. 5.18. *The Alternative.* Frederick O. Seibel, ink, 1947. *Richmond Times-Dispatch,* ALUV.

A rare favorable view of the Truman Doctrine by a political cartoonist.

Fig. 5.19. *Comes Now the Painful Operation.* Jay Norwood (Ding) Darling, ink, 1947. *Des Moines Register,* UIL.

Typical of most political cartoonists, Ding was sympathetic to the Eightieth Congress's efforts to cut Marshall Plan assistance to Europe.

Fig. 5.20. *Sure, Get Right On and Ride Him.* Jay Norwood (Ding) Darling, ink (photostatic reproduction), 1947. *Des Moines Register,* CLDU.

The British mandate of Palestine became a major crisis area by 1947 as thousands of Jews had settled there in their determination to create a Jewish state. In September 1947 a UN committee recommended that two autonomous communities, Arab and Jewish, linked in economic union, be established under UN trusteeship. The Truman administration vacillated between that approach and partition. On May 14, 1948, HST recognized Israeli independence. By the 1950s, continuing Arab-nation resentment led to Soviet assistance. By then the Cold War had turned to that part of the world.

Fig. 5.21. *It Might Have Educational Benefits.* Jay Norwood (Ding) Darling, ink, 1948. *Des Moines Register,* UIL.

The political left and right rejected HST's internationalist, anti-Soviet foreign policy. Ding suggests sending Henry Wallace and conservative Republican House Speaker Joseph Martin, Jr. (Massachusetts) to Russia!

Fig. 5.22. *"Whose Move?"* Walt Kelly, ink, 1948. *New York Star,* HSTL.

Immediately following the Soviet blockade of West Berlin, prospects for war grew more likely. HST met this 1948 challenge by adopting the airlift.

Fig. 5.23. *What's the Hurry?
We've Just Planted This Seed!*
Edward Kuekes, ink, 1949.
Plain Dealer (Cleveland), HSTL.

A military aid program quickly
followed the United States
signing of the NATO treaty. The
Korean War brought on an even
greater United States
commitment to the Atlantic pact.

Fig. 5.24. *We're Behind You Mr.
President, There Was No
Alternative.* Edward Kuekes,
ink, crayon, and opaque white,
1950. *Plain Dealer* (Cleveland),
HSTL.

The intensification of the Cold
War, along with the Soviets
obtaining the atomic bomb,
caused the United States to
develop a superbomb. By 1950
containment moved more in the
direction of a military
commitment.

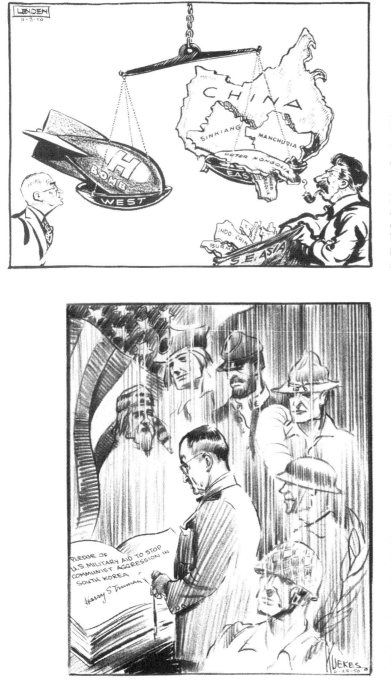

Fig. 5.25. *The Balance.* J. N. Leyden, ink, crayon, and opaque white, 1950. *Natal (South Africa) Daily News,* HSTL.

Leyden wonders what happens after further Communist expansion offsets the precarious balance. Would the United States secure a more potent superbomb as a deterrent?

Fig. 5.26. *Decision.* Edward Kuekes, ink, crayon, and opaque white, 1950. *Plain Dealer* (Cleveland), HSTL.

This cartoon reflects the prevailing public viewpoint. The American people stood behind the president as he quickly responded to the North Korean attack.

Fig. 5.27. *Wrong Kind of Olive Branch.* J. N. Leyden, ink, crayon, and opaque white, 1950. *Natal (South Africa) Daily News,* HSTL.

Another cartoon supporting the Truman administration's Korean intervention.

Fig. 5.28. *United Nations Theme Song.* Frederick O. Seibel, ink, 1950. *Richmond Times-Dispatch,* AWC.

Seibel reflects a rare criticism of Truman's Korean decision in 1950. Although historians remain somewhat divided on that matter today, more credence is given to the view that the Soviet Union did not engineer the invasion. If the Soviet Union had even known of the attack beforehand, would the Russians have boycotted the UN Security Council? A Soviet veto would have hindered UN action. Moreover, some historians contend the North Korean leader, Kim Il Sung, was an avowed nationalist who had often threatened to unite the two Koreas.

Fig. 5.29. *Now for Performances.* John Baer, ink, c. 1951. *Labor,* HSTL.

Although tax increases occurred in this period, HST's patriotic appeal for a "real" excess profits tax failed. The president got little cooperation from the Congress on war-related economic issues.

Fig. 5.30. (*The Best "Defence".*) Don Trachte, ink and watercolor, 1951. Unpublished, HSTL.

In various ways, both editorial and comic-strip cartoonists supported defense bond drives and other patriotic activities. For example, in November 1951 National Cartoonist Society members breakfasted with HST in the Carlton Hotel in Washington, D.C. They were there to help the Treasury Department sell defense stamps. They also presented HST with a bound volume of cartoons. Along with the Henry cartoon, the following represent some of their drawings.

Fig. 5.31. (*The Best Medicine.*) Zeke Zekley, ink and colored crayon, 1951. Unpublished, HSTL.

Zekley was a gag illustrator.

Fig. 5.32. "*Confidentially, Harry . . .* " Vaughn Shoemaker, ink and watercolor, 1951. Unpublished, HSTL.

Shoemaker was an editorial cartoonist.

Fig. 5.33. *"We'll All Lend a Hand!"* Leonard D. Warren, ink and gouache, 1951. Unpublished, HSTL.

Warren, an editorial cartoonist, also contributed to the breakfast volume.

Fig. 5.34. *"Will You Run Again . . . ?"* Leonard Sansone, ink and watercolor, 1951. *Life,* HSTL.

The Sansone cartoon was among those printed in the December 6, 1951, issue of *Life* that covered the cartoon breakfast.

Fig. 5.35. (*A Mighty Trio*.) Bob Kane, ink and watercolor, 1951. Unpublished, HSTL.

Bob Kane did most of his work in comic books.

Fig. 5.36. *The People Are Proud of Their Chief*. John Baer, ink, c. 1950. *Labor,* HSTL.

By early fall of 1950 the North Koreans had been pushed back. It appeared that the war would soon be over. Consequently, HST could better refute the Republican charge that his administration was soft on Communism.

Fig. 5.37. *A Welcome Relief from the Main Bout.* Richard Yardley, ink and benday film, 1950. *Sun* (Baltimore), AWC.

This cartoon represents a common theme. Yardley proposes that while HST challenged music critic Hume, he refused to battle "Uncle Joe" Stalin and Mao Tse-tung whose Chinese forces had now entered the Korean War.

Fig. 5.38. *Not a Pleasant Outlook for Me.* Edwin Marcus, ink, 1950. *New York Times,* LC.

The above depicts HST's meeting with General MacArthur at the famous Wake Island Conference of October 15, 1950. There, MacArthur advised the president that the Chinese would not intervene in Korea. If they did, he said, they would be "slaughtered." The following month Chinese troops intervened en masse.

Fig. 5.39. (*A Loose Fit.*) John Chase, ink and benday film, 1950. *New Orleans States,* LC.

MacArthur's service cap is too big for HST. Chase obviously favors the general in the emerging clash of the two leaders. Truman never cared for MacArthur. As early as 1945, he referred to him as "Mr. Prima Donna, Brass Hat, Five Star MacArthur. He's worse than the Cabots and the Lodges — they at least talked with one another before they told God what to do. Mac tells God right off," HST wrote.

Fig. 5.40. *The Mouth of the Big Gun.* Cyrus Hungerford, ink, 1951. *Pittsburgh Post-Gazette,* AWC.

After the Chinese intervention, MacArthur publicly criticized the president for seeking a diplomatic settlement in Korea. HST, believing United States vital interests were in Europe, was more anxious to strengthen NATO forces that Eisenhower commanded.

Fig. 5.41. *Gulliver and the Lilliputians.* Ferman Martin, ink, crayon, and graphite, 1951. *Houston Chronicle,* SHSM.

Another portrayal of the Truman-MacArthur controversy, Martin criticizes the president for preventing the general from achieving military victory in Korea. MacArthur sought to bomb strategic installations in China, impose a naval blockade against that country, and "unleash" Chiang Kai-shek from Formosa. All of this, HST believed, would embroil the United States in a general war involving the Soviet Union.

Fig. 5.42. *When Is He Going to Fade Away?* Frederick O. Seibel, ink and opaque white, 1951. *Richmond Times-Dispatch,* AWC.

The polls revealed that Americans overwhelmingly sided with MacArthur. The general was a hero to most Americans. Moreover, his total victory beliefs were more appealing than HST's limited-war policy, which most people probably did not understand. Historians, however, have vindicated Truman.

Fig. 5.43. *Big Step in Good Neighbor Policy.* Herc Ficklen, ink, crayon, and opaque white, 1951. *Dallas Morning News,* HSTL.

During the Korean War, the Truman administration negotiated an agreement with Mexico, enabling Mexican braceros ("hired hands"), working in the Southwest, to receive prevailing wages established by the secretary of labor. The agreement in other ways regulated bracero use. This matter had been a sore point between the two governments. The Mexicans felt that American growers had exploited Mexican migrant workers. The United States, meanwhile, was concerned about the large migration of Mexicans into the country.

Fig. 5.44. *You Wouldn't Hide Anything from Us Would You, Harry?* Jay Norwood (Ding) Darling, ink (photostatic reproduction), 1948. *Des Moines Register,* ALDU.

The Cold War also existed on the domestic front. As early as 1945, the Truman administration faced FBI and congressional inquiries intent on exposing Communist infiltration in the federal service. Moreover, the Republican Eightieth Congress sought to embarrass the president. The almost hysterical public mood encouraged the Red-baiting.

Fig. 5.45. *" . . . I'll Fix It for You in November!"* Gib Crockett, ink and benday film, c. 1948. *Washington Star,* AWC.

HST responded in various ways to the Communist-in-government charges. For example, in 1947 he established a loyalty program designed to expunge Communists and their fellow travelers from the government. Politically speaking, the effort failed. The Republican congressional opposition remained skeptical and critical. Crockett's cartoon represents one example of this.

Fig. 5.46. *"There Are No Communists . . . "* Wills Scott Shadburne, ink, c. 1948. *Springfield (Missouri) Leader and Press,* HSTL.

Shadburne's criticism of HST's anticommunist efforts is a typical example of the emotional press coverage of the time.

Fig. 5.47. *Something Fishy, All Right.* Burris Jenkins, ink, crayon, and opaque white, 1948. *New York Journal-American,* HSTL.

Prior to McCarthy, Truman's greatest nemesis on the Communist-in-government issue was the House Committee on Un-American Activities. In 1948 its investigations cast a shadow of suspicion on several former and current federal employees including William Remington of the Commerce Department and Alger Hiss, formerly of the State Department. HST dismissed the Republican-controlled House committee's charges as politically inspired. At a 1948 press conference, he even labeled the allegations a "red herring."

Fig. 5.48. *The Tried and the Triumvirate.* Joseph Parrish, ink and watercolor (clipping from *Chicago Tribune,* copyright © 1950).

The most damaging charge the House Committee on Un-American Activities made against the Democratic party was that Alger Hiss had been a Communist agent. The well-educated and suave Hiss was a prototypical New Deal liberal, enabling administration critics to indict the liberal establishment. Secretary of State Dean Acheson, by being a character witness at the Hiss trial, assisted that process. HST too was judged guilty by association.

Fig. 5.49. *A Red Herring, Mr. President?* Edward Kuekes, ink (clipping from *Plain Dealer* [Cleveland], 1950).

HST's red-herring statement came back to haunt him and the party following Hiss's conviction in 1950. For years, however, liberals questioned the "weak" circumstantial evidence that accompanied Hiss's conviction. Today there is more reason for believing him guilty.

Fig. 5.50. *Old Ghosts Never Die.* Herc Ficklen, ink and crayon, 1953. *Dallas Morning News,* HSTL.

The Hiss case continued to follow HST in later years. The Chambers documents pertained to the microfilmed documentary evidence that former Communist Whittaker Chambers presented to implicate Hiss. Chambers had concealed the evidence in a hollowed-out pumpkin on his Maryland farm.

Fig. 5.51. *Disgraceful.* Bruce Russell, ink, crayon, and opaque white, 1954. *Los Angeles Herald,* HSTL.

Russell criticizes HST for his negative appraisal of the Joseph McCarthy-inspired congressional investigation of the army in 1954.

6

PRESIDENT EMERITUS

ON INAUGURATION DAY of 1953, after nearly eight tumultuous years as chief executive, Harry Truman relinquished the presidency to Dwight David Eisenhower. HST, Bess, and Margaret immediately returned to their Victorian house in Independence, Missouri, where the former president adopted the role of Mr. Citizen. But as Truman soon learned, ex-presidents are more than private citizens. The local community too often views them as approximating royalty. Moreover, party leaders and government officials still seek their assistance, while Americans everywhere look to them for patriarchical wisdom. Until fragile health or old age intervenes, most former presidents willingly assume active roles.

Few twentieth-century ex-presidents were more active than Truman. He in fact did much to strengthen the ex-presidency, an institution in its own right. He spent the first years of "retirement" writing his presidential *Memoirs*. When the final volume was published in 1956, Truman had already regained much of the popularity he lost late in his presidency. The following year he officially dedicated the Harry S. Truman presidential library after having raised private funds to construct the contemporary building about one-half mile from his Independence home. It is in that library that his private and public correspondence is housed.

As a needed distraction in this period, the Trumans managed several vacations. In the summer of 1953, after an Hawaii sojourn that spring, the former president and Bess drove to Washington, D.C., to visit friends. They soon learned, following countless distractions, that they could not travel like ordinary Americans. Three years later the Trumans embarked on a European trip, including a visit to England where Truman received an honorary degree from Oxford University. In 1959 he even ventured to New York City, a frequent haunt, to be a guest on the Jack Benny TV show. The Trumans' private lives were also enriched by the marriage of Margaret to *New York Times* editor Clifton Daniel in 1956. Editorial cartoonists affectionately responded to the wedding as they would in 1957 to the birth of the first grandson, Clifton Truman Daniel.

But the early postpresidential years represented a time of frustration for Truman. He had always believed that former presidents were peculiarly well-equipped to provide useful bipartisan service. He proved that in his own presidency by resurrecting Herbert Hoover whom Franklin Roosevelt had ignored. In 1953 Truman hoped that he would be called upon by President Eisenhower to play the role of elder statesman. An invitation to serve never came, causing Truman to label Ike the "White House Bonehead." No wonder writers and editorial cartoonists of the 1950s referred to a Truman-Eisenhower "feud."

The feud began in the heated presidential campaign of 1952 when Eisenhower failed to defend his former military superior, General George Marshall, from the McCarthyite attacks of Republican Senators McCarthy and Albert Jenner (Indiana). Marshall had been Truman's secretary of state, a person Truman greatly admired, and he felt that Eisenhower had treated Marshall very badly. The Truman-Eisenhower relationship worsened after Eisenhower's attorney general, Herbert Brownell, Jr., accused Truman of knowingly betraying the security of the United States as president, causing the Republican-controlled House Committee on Un-American Activities to subpoena him and other former administration officials. As some political cartoonists suggested, the feud lessened somewhat after Ike's presidency. More immediately, it intensified Truman's partisan criticism of the Eisenhower administration. Only during foreign policy crises did Truman back the president.

In his relations with Congress, Truman fared better as elder statesman. Congressional committees sought his wisdom on pending legislation. He responded by testifying before various congressional subcommittees, by writing letters, and by issuing informal statements. Truman also used his influence over the Democratic congressional leadership to elevate the ex-presidency. A 1958 bill, for example, provided former presidents with franking privileges, a $25,000 annual allowance, a staff stipend, and office space and furnishings.

Truman's efforts as party leader represented successes and failings. As a former president, he retained considerable political influence. The limitations were also imposing, for he no longer controlled the instruments of power. But what strengthened his position was Adlai Stevenson's reluctance to assume party leadership following the 1952 election and Truman's own political resurgence by the mid-1950s. Consequently, Democratic candidates successfully sought Truman's participation in various congressional and presidential campaigns from 1954 through 1962. His buoyant, self-confident, "give-em-hell Harry" style remained an inspiration to those who remembered 1948. And there is no question that his pugnacious speeches helped carry Democratic candidates to victory.

Truman's shortcomings and lack of power were more evident when he sought to impose his presidential candidates upon the Democratic national conventions. At the Chicago convention in 1956 amid an overflowing press conference, he dramatically endorsed the liberal governor of New York, Averell Harriman, even though Stevenson clearly remained the delegates' overwhelming choice, as the first ballot nomination soon revealed. To Truman's credit, he campaigned strongly for Stevenson that fall. In 1960 Truman again challenged the Democratic front-runner, John F. Kennedy, who swept the primaries. He backed Stuart Symington, a fellow Missourian, for the party nomination. Truman's opposition to Kennedy was no doubt due to the latter's failure to support the Truman administration's China policy, his grasping father, his family's ties with McCarthy, his youth and inexperience, and his Catholicism. But once again, Truman had to downplay his denunciation of a successful party nominee as he prepared for the fall campaign. He nonetheless campaigned vigorously for JFK against Richard Nixon whom he loathed. Truman in time came to respect President Kennedy. But his relationship with JFK's successor, Lyndon Baines Johnson, was much closer. They had worked together politically in the 1950s when Johnson became Democratic leader in the Senate. Truman strongly favored LBJ's presidential nomination in 1964; he would have campaigned for him that fall. By then, however, old age complicated by a serious fall in the bathroom forced Truman into near retirement as a public figure.

In the Kennedy-Johnson years, Truman remained out-spoken on key public issues. Only rarely, however, did his advice have much impact. His once liberal views on civil rights were now out of touch with the more activist sentiment of the 1960s. Truman lambasted the sit-ins and the freedom riders and publicly labeled Martin Luther King, Jr., a troublemaker, to the satisfaction of the southern leadership. In 1966 he publicly criticized the Johnson administration for its economic policies, arguing that high interest rates would lead to a depression. Johnson disagreed. Yet he continued to identify with Truman's presidency as he traveled to Independence in 1965 to sign the Medicare bill. Twenty years earlier Truman had first advocated a comprehensive national health insurance measure. Johnson also depended on Truman for public support for his Vietnam policy. More than this, President Truman's courageous steadfastness in the face of public criticism during the Korean War helped to sustain Johnson as he confronted the Vietnam War opposition.

By the close of Johnson's presidency, political cartoonists accurately revealed a visibly aging and fragile Truman who nonetheless continued to be an inspiration to political candidates, especially to Hubert H. Humphrey in 1968. In Truman's last years, political cartoonists responded sympathetically to his hospital stays and birthdays. On December 26, 1972, at age eighty-eight, Truman died. As did so many others, the cartoonists paid their final respects, as a warm relationship had now ended.

Fig. 6.1. *There Goes Harry — "He Done His Damndest."* Frederick O. Seibel, ink, 1953. *Richmond Times-Dispatch,* ALUV.

Mr. President becomes Mr. Citizen.

Fig. 6.2. *The Rewrite Man.* Bruce Russell, ink and crayon (clipping from *Los Angeles Herald*), 1955.

Some cartoonists suggested that Truman distorted historical fact in his writings. Indeed, most presidential memoirs are mere self-justification. Truman's two volumes, however, were for the most part well received.

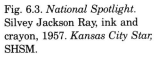

Fig. 6.3. *National Spotlight.* Silvey Jackson Ray, ink and crayon, 1957. *Kansas City Star,* SHSM.

Truman was the first ex-president to establish a presidential library. Today it remains a major source for historical inquiry. Moreover, more than 250,000 Americans visit the library museum annually.

Fig. 6.4. *Tourist Season.* Gib Crockett, ink and benday film, 1953. *Washington Star,* HSTL.

Whether intended or not, the above cartoon is wonderfully symbolic. The "nation's No. 1 tourist" stayed outside the White House in Eisenhower's presidency. Kennedy made Truman his first White House guest even though he rarely consulted him.

Fig. 6.5. *Harry! — What a Hat!*
Leo Joseph Roche, ink, crayon,
and opaque white, 1956. *Buffalo
Courier-Express,* HSTL.

Truman's honorary degree was a
Doctor of Civil Law. He was
actually one of two twentieth-
century presidents who never
graduated from college.

Fig. 6.6. *The Old Trouper.* Herc
Ficklen, ink, 1959. *Dallas
Morning News,* HSTL.

Truman's TV appearance
brought forth some criticism
that he was humiliating his
great office. In an unsent letter,
Truman suggested to one critic
that "if your humiliation puts
you too far in the mud maybe I
can pull you out before you
smother. It might help if you
weren't pulled out!"

Fig. 6.7. *Come Children, Mr. Truman Is Talking to Reporters!* Joseph Parrish, ink (clipping from *Chicago Tribune,* copyright © 1955).

Outside one of New York City's hotels, a visiting HST responds in a salty manner to reporters' questions.

Fig. 6.8. *Father of the Bride.* James Berryman, ink and crayon, 1956. *Washington Star,* HSTL.

Given to impromptu press conferences on sundry political matters, Truman was ordered by the Truman ladies not to upstage Margaret's wedding.

Fig. 6.9. *"Look at It This Way, Harry . . . "* John Chase, ink and benday film, 1956. *New Orleans States,* HSTL.

Even though friends kidded him about it, Harry never had any problems with this newspaperman. He and Clifton Daniel had a warm relationship with the latter affectionately referring to his father-in-law as grandpa.

Fig. 6.10. *Maybe He's Not Kidding.* James Berryman, ink and benday film, 1957. *Washington Star,* HSTL.

Truman had to review those books four times, for he had four grandsons: Clifton Truman, William, Harrison, and Thomas. Besides the cartoon's explanation, he had other reasons for rejecting Dulles's invitation to visit Greece and Turkey. Those two countries had extended an invitation via the Eisenhower government to commemorate the tenth anniversary of the Truman Doctrine. Dulles only belatedly asked Truman to attend.

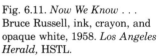

Fig. 6.11. *Now We Know . . .*
Bruce Russell, ink, crayon, and
opaque white, 1958. *Los Angeles
Herald,* HSTL.

Although Truman often visited
his grandsons in New York, it is
doubtful that he gave them their
bottle.

Fig. 6.12. *Here Lies the Hatchet.*
Wills Scott Shadburne, ink,
1952. *Springfield (Missouri)
Leader and Press,* HSTL.

Truman indeed went after Ike in
the 1952 presidential campaign.
In a Colorado Springs speech, he
argued that Ike's unwillingness to
defend General Marshall made
him unworthy to be president.

Fig. 6.13. *And Friday the Thirteenth, Too.* Joseph Parrish, ink, 1953. Copyright © *Chicago Tribune,* AWC.

In 1953 Republican Attorney General Herbert Brownell, Jr., charged that President Truman had appointed Assistant Secretary of the Treasury Harry Dexter White to the Board of Directors of the International Monetary Fund despite receiving a FBI report that White was a Communist. Consequently, the House Committee on Un-American Activities subpoenaed Truman. He refused to honor the subpoena. Believing that Republicans sought to embarrass him, he argued that the subpoena abridged the doctrine of separation of powers, threatening the independence of the presidency. He was the first former president to extend executive privilege to the ex-presidency.

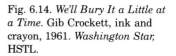

Fig. 6.14. *We'll Bury It a Little at a Time.* Gib Crockett, ink and crayon, 1961. *Washington Star,* HSTL.

There was some reconciliation in 1961. The two visited at the Truman library. Two years later the Eisenhowers lunched with Truman at Blair House after John Kennedy's funeral.

Fig. 6.15. *There Are Ghosts on Old Ships*. James Berryman, ink and benday film, 1953. *Washington Star,* HSTL.

As the cartoon implies, Truman almost relished his role as critic of Eisenhower's domestic policies.

Fig. 6.16. *Takes One to Know One*. Bill McClanahan, ink and crayon, 1957. *Dallas Morning News,* HSTL.

The anti-Truman cartoon nonetheless correctly reveals Truman's critical appraisal of Eisenhower's secretary of state, John Foster Dulles.

Fig. 6.17. *Other Fellow's Ox.* Bill McClanahan, ink, crayon, and opaque white, 1958. *Dallas Morning News,* HSTL.

McClanahan accuses Truman of hypocrisy in his deploring of the Sherman Adams scandal that led to the dismissal of Ike's chief of staff.

Fig. 6.18. *Unexpected Boost.* Leo Joseph Roche, ink and crayon (clipping from *Buffalo Courier-Express),* 1955.

Believing in a bipartisan foreign policy, Truman generally supported the Eisenhower foreign policy initiatives particularly in crisis situations. He strongly urged congressional approval of the Eisenhower Doctrine of 1957 for the troubled Middle East.

Fig. 6.19. *It's All Yours Governor.*
Herc Ficklen, ink, crayon, and
opaque white, 1953. *Dallas
Morning News,* HSTL.

After his 1952 election defeat,
the aloof Stevenson walked
away from party leadership,
leaving Truman to play a more
active party role.

Fig. 6.20. *Can Hurricane Harry
Bowl Him Over?* Frederick O.
Seibel, ink, 1954. *Richmond
Times-Dispatch,* HSTL.

Truman played little part in the
1954 congressional campaign
after emergency gallbladder
surgery.

Fig. 6.21. *And That's That!* Leo Joseph Roche, ink, crayon, and opaque white, c. 1956. *Buffalo Courier-Express,* HSTL.

There was some speculation that Truman might accept second place on a 1956 Stevenson ticket. Nothing, of course, came of this.

Fig. 6.22. *Seems to Have 'Em Worried.* Leo Joseph Roche, ink and crayon, 1955. *Buffalo Courier-Express,* HSTL.

One of the political cartoonists' most common themes regarding Truman's postpresidential campaigning was the 1948 reference.

Fig. 6.23. *All Set*. Mike Parks, ink and benday film, 1956. *San Francisco Examiner,* HSTL.

The Parks cartoon humorously suggests that Truman would have something to say about the 1956 Democratic presidential campaign. As it turned out, he did have a hand in shaping the party platform.

Fig. 6.24. *Scene Stealer.* Reg Manning, ink and crayon, 1955. *Arizona Republic* (Phoenix), HSTL.

Truman made quite a splash at the 1956 party convention in Chicago, attracting 800 reporters at his opening press conference.

Fig. 6.25. *In the Spotlight.*
Franklin Osborne Alexander,
ink and crayon, 1956.
Philadelphia Bulletin, HSTL.

Yet another cartoon that shows
HST in the convention limelight.

Fig. 6.26. *In a Horse-Filled
Room.* Daniel Fitzpatrick, ink,
crayon, and opaque white, 1956.
St. Louis Post-Dispatch, HSTL.

As this well-conceived cartoon
suggests, the perplexed Truman
confused popularity and power
at Chicago. Former presidents
have little of the latter.
Obviously, Truman was unable
to control the party horses at the
convention. The result was
Stevenson's nomination.

Fig. 6.27. *Me? Look Like a Candidate? Heh Heh Heh!* Jack Knox, ink and crayon, 1956. *Nashville Banner,* HSTL.

Adlai Stevenson and his running mate, Senator Estes Kefauver of Tennessee, appear frightened by the prospects of Truman's aggressive and independent campaigning.

Fig. 6.28. *The Old Fire Horse.* Daniel Dowling, ink, crayon, and opaque white, 1958. *New York Herald-Tribune,* HSTL.

In the 1958 congressional campaign, Truman delivered twenty-five major speeches in at least twenty different states.

Fig. 6.29. *How Come He's Still Pitching?* Reg Manning, ink and crayon, 1958. *Arizona Republic* (Phoenix), HSTL.

Another view of HST the campaigner in 1958.

Fig. 6.30. *You Can See for Yourself Who's the Strongest Candidate.* Edward Valtman, ink and benday film, 1960. *Hartford (Connecticut) Times,* HSTL.

In 1960 Truman overestimated the chances of his candidate, Senator Stuart Symington of Missouri, winning the Democratic nomination.

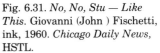

Fig. 6.31. *No, No, Stu — Like This.* Giovanni (John) Fischetti, ink, 1960. *Chicago Daily News,* HSTL.

As the cartoon suggests, Symington's nomination bid never really gained momentum.

Fig. 6.32. *Just Leave the Bottle There, Bartender.* Bruce Russell, ink and crayon, 1960. *Los Angeles Herald,* HSTL.

Russell highlights Truman's criticism of Kennedy's youth and inexperience.

Fig. 6.33. *Another Fourth of July Casualty.* Edward Valtman, ink and benday film, 1960. *Hartford (Connecticut) Times,* HSTL.

On the first ballot, the Kennedy steamroller overwhelmed Truman (and Symington *et al.*) at the Democratic National Convention in Los Angeles. Anticipating the result, Truman decided not to attend the convention as a delegate.

Fig. 6.34. *"When I Make Statements . . . !"* Bill McClanahan, ink and benday film, 1960. *Dallas Morning News,* HSTL.

After Kennedy's nomination, Truman had to eat crow as he endorsed the party nominee.

Fig. 6.35. *Kennedy, Kennedy, Rah-Rah-Rah.* Robbie Robinson, ink and crayon, 1960. *Indianapolis News,* HSTL.

Another lukewarm supporter was Eleanor Roosevelt who preferred Stevenson in 1960.

Fig. 6.36. *And of Course Harry Will Accompany.* Vaughn Shoemaker, ink, crayon, and opaque white, 1960. *Chicago Daily News,* HSTL.

Truman eventually campaigned strongly for Kennedy that fall, particularly in the South and Midwest.

Fig. 6.37. *The 11th Commandment.* Charles G. Werner, ink and crayon, 1960. *Indianapolis Star,* HSTL.

One reason for Truman's active support of Kennedy is aptly explained in the above cartoon. There was perhaps no opponent whom Truman disliked more. The reason for this goes back to the 1952 campaign when Nixon supposedly called him a traitor.

Fig. 6.38. *That Boy Is Acting More Like a President Every Day.* James Berryman, ink and crayon, 1963. *Washington Star,* HSTL.

The above cartoon symbolizes the growing affection Truman had for President Kennedy. John Diefenbaker was the Canadian Prime Minister whom Kennedy obviously disliked.

Fig. 6.39. *And I Thought He Wasn't Up to the Job!* James Berryman, ink and crayon, 1962. *Washington Star,* JFKL.

Even though JFK failed to get the Medicare bill through Congress, HST admired his fighting spirit.

Fig. 6.40. *Bess, I'm Going Out for a Walk. . . .* Paul Conrad, ink, crayon, and opaque white, 1964. Copyright © *Los Angeles Times,* HSTL.

Although strongly endorsing LBJ in 1964, Truman found Johnson's politics of harmony not particularly appealing.

Fig. 6.41. (*Ready To Respond.*) Bill McClanahan, ink and crayon, 1964. *Dallas Morning News,* HSTL.

HST was indeed ready but unable to campaign in 1964.

Fig. 6.42. *Aw, H . . . , They Said the Same Thing About Me, Remember?* Robbie Robinson, ink, crayon, and opaque white, 1964. *Indianapolis News,* HSTL.

Cartoonists often identified presidential underdogs like Barry Goldwater with Truman and 1948.

Fig. 6.43. *Thanks, Harry.* Bill McClanahan, ink, crayon, and opaque white, 1961. *Dallas Morning News*, HSTL.

A favorable cartoon of Truman's law and order approach to the civil rights movement of the early 1960s.

Fig. 6.44. *In Three Volumes, Read Them Over Carefully!* Jerry Doyle, ink, crayon, and opaque white, 1966. *Philadelphia Daily News*, SHSM.

Truman was concerned about the United States economy in the mid-1960s. What occurred, however, was not deflation. As President Johnson escalated the Vietnam War without increasing taxes, a long period of inflation set in.

Fig. 6.45. *Signing It for Harry.*
Cyrus Hungerford, ink, 1965.
Pittsburgh Post-Gazette, HSTL.

Truman's national health
insurance program was much
more comprehensive than the
Medicare Bill of 1965.

Fig. 6.46. *Things Haven't
Changed So Much.* William W.
Sanders, ink and crayon, 1965.
Kansas City Star, HSTL.

Johnson wrote Truman in this
period: "Not a day passes that I
am not sustained in our struggle
for peace by the bright memories
of your own courageous stands
and great successes in that
cause."

Fig. 6.47. *I Believe You've Got the Hang of It.* William W. Sanders, ink and crayon, 1964. *Kansas City Star,* HSTL.

Truman was at the Democratic National Convention of 1968 only in spirit, but that spirit was strong!

Fig. 6.48. (*Tell Me Again How You Did It.*) Gene B. McCarty, ink, crayon, and opaque white, 1968. *Sun-Telegram* (San Bernardino, California), HSTL.

A cartoonist again adopts the 1948 analogy as Hubert Humphrey fell behind in the polls.

Fig. 6.49. *Well Sonovabitch . . . Welcome to the Club.* Gene B. McCarty, ink and benday film, 1970. *Sun-Telegram* (San Bernardino, California), HSTL.

Why McCarty linked Ronald Reagan with Truman on the eve of the 1970 California gubernatorial election is unclear. Perhaps he viewed Reagan as an underdog who nevertheless would win.

Fig. 6.50. *(Following Harry's Advice.)* James Burnett Ivey, ink and crayon, 1970. Copyright © *Orlando Evening Star,* HSTL.

At least one cartoonist compared Vice-President Spiro Agnew's invectives to HST's "give-em-hell-Harry" style.

Fig. 6.51. *The New Recruit.*
Gene B. McCarty, ink, crayon,
and graphite, 1969.
Sun-Telegram (San Bernardino,
California), HSTL.

At Ike's inauguration in 1953,
Herbert Hoover had joked to
Truman: "We ought to organize a
former President's club." Truman
responded, "Fine, you be the
president and I will be the
secretary." In 1964 Hoover died.
Five years later, LBJ joined
Truman and Eisenhower.

Fig. 6.52. *I Am Not a
Republican, But You Still Have
to Have a Shot.* William W.
Sanders, ink and crayon, 1964.
Kansas City Star, HSTL.

In 1964 Truman was
hospitalized for cracked ribs
following a bathroom fall.

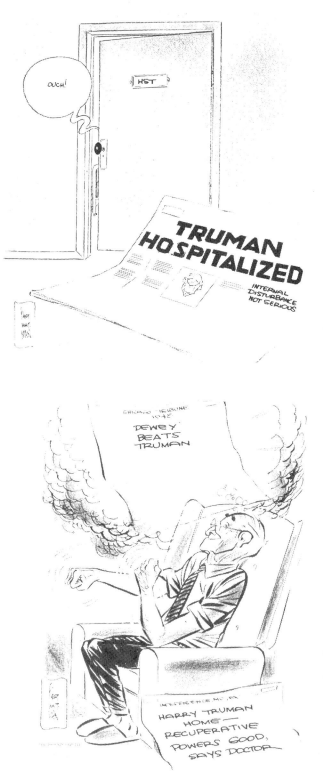

Fig. 6.53. *His Calmest Comment on Record.* Bert Whitman, ink, crayon, and opaque white, 1966. *Stockton (California) Record,* HSTL.

In 1966 HST was again in the hospital after suffering dizzy spells that forced him to discontinue his daily walks.

Fig. 6.54. *I've Put Up Good Fights Before.* Bert Whitman, ink and crayon, 1971. *Phoenix Gazette,* HSTL.

Various illnesses continued to plague the former president. In his last years he became considerably enfeebled.

Fig. 6.55. *Going like 60 — at 75.* Lou Grant, ink and crayon, 1959. *Oakland Tribune,* HSTL.

At age seventy-five, Truman indeed was going strong.

Fig. 6.56. *Give 'Em Hell, Harry.* Lou Grant, ink, crayon, opaque white, and benday film, 1964. *Oakland Tribune,* HSTL.

About five months after his eightieth birthday that terrible fall occurred.

Fig. 6.57. *I Just Stopped By to Wish You a Happy 83rd Birthday.* William W. Sanders, ink and crayon, 1967. *Kansas City Star,* SHSM.

At eighty-three HST still had hopes of reaching ninety.

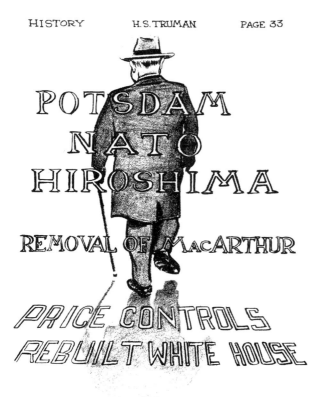

Fig. 6.58. (*The History Maker.*) Bill Roberts, ink and crayon, 1972. *Cleveland Press,* HSTL.

One of many cartoons that praised Truman at his death. This cartoon is nonetheless a misguided effort. It seems strange to praise HST for Hiroshima in 1972. And was the rebuilding of the White House a major accomplishment of his presidency? Why weren't the Marshall Plan and the desegregation of the armed forces instead included?

Fig. 6.59. (*The Last Waltz.*) Gib Crockett, ink and crayon, 1972. Copyright © *Washington Star-News,* HSTL.

Although this cartoon represented a popular theme, Truman detested the Missouri Waltz.

Fig. 6.60. *A Fighter to the End.* James Arthur (Art) Wood, Jr., ink, crayon, and opaque white, 1972. *Richmond News Leader,* HSTL.

This cartoon needs no explanation. Truman is still remembered as a fighter for the people.

Truman-related Works

Donovan, Robert J. *Conflict and Crisis: The Presidency of Harry S. Truman, 1945–1948*. New York: Norton, 1977.
_____. *Tumultuous Years: The Presidency of Harry S. Truman, 1949–1953*. New York: Norton, 1982.
Ferrell, Robert H. *Harry S. Truman and the Modern American Presidency*. Boston: Little, Brown, 1983.
_____, ed. *Off the Record: The Private Papers of Harry S. Truman*. New York: Harper and Row, 1980.
_____, ed. *The Autobiography of Harry S. Truman*. Boulder: Colorado Associated Univ. Press, Univ. Colorado Press, 1980.
Giglio, James N. "Harry S. Truman and the Multifarious Ex-Presidency," *Presidential Studies Quarterly* 12: (Spring 1982): 239–55.
Gosnell, Harold F. *Truman's Crises: A Political Biography of Harry S. Truman*. Westport, Conn.: Greenwood, 1980.
Hamby, Alonzo. *Beyond the New Deal: Harry S. Truman and American Liberalism*. New York: Columbia Univ. Press, 1973.
Truman, Harry S. *Memoirs: Year of Decisions*. Garden City, N. Y.: Doubleday, 1955.
_____. *Memoirs: Years of Trial and Hope*. Garden City, N. Y.: Doubleday, 1956.
Truman, Margaret. *Harry S. Truman*. New York: Morrow, 1973.
Underhill, Robert. *The Truman Persuasions*. Ames: Iowa State Univ. Press, 1981.

Political Cartoon-related Works

Dennis, Everette E. "The Regeneration of Political Cartooning," *Journalism Quarterly* 60 (Winter 1974): 664–69.
Foreign Policy Association Editors, eds. *A Cartoon History of United States Foreign Policy, 1776–1976*. New York: Morrow, 1975.
Hess, Stephen, and Kaplan, Milton. *The Ungentlemanly Art: A History of American Political Cartoons*. New York: Macmillan, 1968.
Hoff, Syd. *Editorial and Political Cartooning*. New York: Stravon Educational Press, 1976.
Horn, Maurice, ed. *The World Encyclopedia of Cartoons*. 2 vols. New York: Chelsea House Publishers, 1980.
Lendt, David L. *Ding: The Life of Jay Norwood Darling*. Ames: Iowa State Univ. Press, 1979.
Lucie-Smith, Edward. *The Art of Caricature*. Ithaca, N.Y.: Cornell Univ. Press, 1981.
Tarter, Brent, and Kukla, Jon. "Fred Seibel," *Virginia Cavalcade* (Spring 1977): 148–61.